This book is designed to provide information that the author believes to be accurate on the subject matter covered and is sold with the understanding that it is not equivalent to the author nor the publisher offering individualized advice on any specific portfolio, or any individual's particular needs. Neither does the book offer investment advice or other professional services such as legal and or accounting services. Professional advice should be sought in areas that include investment, legal and accounting advice. The book also references performance data collected over many periods. Past results do not guarantee future performance.

In addition, performance data, in addition to laws and regulations, evolve over time, which could change the status of the information in this publication. This book also provides historical data to discuss and illustrate the underlying principles and hence it is not intended to serve as a basis for financial decisions, specific recommendation of a specific investment advisor, or an offer to sell or buy securities. Only a prospectus may be used to offer to sell or purchase any securities, and a prospectus must be read and considered carefully before investing or spending money. No warranty is made with respect to the accuracy or completeness of the information contained in this book, and both the author and the publisher specifically disclaim any responsibility for any liability, loss, or risk, personal or otherwise, which is incurred as a result, directly or indirectly, of the use and application of one of the contents in this book.

Legal disclosure; The author owns some of the securities discussed in the book but did not receive compensation for mentioning those securities in this book.

Also by Isaac Jonas

The Basics of Investing in the Stock market online course available on
www.streetwiseeconomics.com

The Intelligent Millennial Investor

Personal Finance and Investing Tips for Millennial Investors

Isaac Jonas

B.Sc. Hons., University of Zimbabwe, 2010

MFRE, University of British Columbia, 2015

M.A. in RES, University of British Columbia, 2021

For

My parents who brought me into this world.

My wife who supports me through the ups and downs of life and our son we recently welcomed.

The millions of Millennial Investors across the world, who are part of the digital revolution and who aspire to build lasting wealth and happiness.

Contents

Contents

The Intelligent Millennial Investor 3

Personal Finance and Investing Tips for Millennial Investors 3

Foreword 6

Chapter 1: Introduction 7

Chapter 2: The Essence of Specific Education in Building Wealth 15

Chapter 3: Understanding debt 23

Chapter 4: Building Savings 39

Chapter 5: The basics of the stock market 56

Chapter 6: How to pick stocks for investing 76

Chapter 7: Portfolio diversification 99

Chapter 8: Estate planning 109

Appreciation 116

About the author 117

Glossary 120

List of Abbreviations 122

Cited Sources 123

Foreword

I am a practicing physician and an immigrant to the United States. It was at the very beginning of my journey to becoming a doctor that I met the author Isaac Jonas at the University of Zimbabwe in 2006. Although we met during a time of great uncertainty, political unrest, and economic turmoil in Zimbabwe, it was through these circumstances that a great friendship was born. We both immigrated to North America to pursue higher education at different times but continued to stay in touch. Since I have come to know Isaac for almost seventeen years, I can summarize his character as a selfless man of ambition, tenacity and above all – integrity.

The intelligent millennial investor, *Personal Finance, and Investing Tips for Millennials* is a testament to Isaac's dedication in making financial literacy and knowledge accessible to everyone.

It is important to note that even though this book is written from an immigrant's perspective, its principles are applicable to people from all walks of life. As one goes through the book, it becomes apparent that the author managed to distill the complicated financial concepts in such a way that the reader is left empowered to act.

This book is a great easy read for anyone who wants to understand the complicated world of financial investments and the instruments that exist to those who want to achieve financial independence. It is a well written, accurate text that not only imparts facts, but life lessons that have been shown by time immemorial to be tested and true means for accumulating wealth. I highly recommend The Intelligent Millennial Investor, *Personal Finance, and Investing Tips for Millennials* not only because of the valuable principles described in the book, but also the genuine intent of the author to help everyone reach financial independence and prosperity.

Sincerely,

Emmanuel Magara, MD

Chapter 1: Introduction

When I was growing up, I was taught that money is everything and I must work hard for it. As a result, I spent most of my childhood working hard on everything I did with the overall goal of becoming rich one day. I hoped that being rich would solve all the problems in my life circle. Two decades ago, like most millennials of my age around the world trying to find the meaning of life and build wealth, I imagined what wealth would bring. To me, back then, it meant a big, beautiful house in the leafy suburbs of my native Zimbabwe, a net worth of at least a million dollars in my bank account and the ability to afford nice cars. From an early age, I fancied driving a Mercedes Benz, as it was seen as a symbol of wealth in my Zimbabwean community. All in all, I spent a great deal of time imagining how it would feel to be wealthy. To add more fuel to my imagination, each time I switched on a television, I would be bombarded with adverts of brand-new cars showing how amazing it is to own one. Perhaps back then I was too young and naive to think through a maze of complex issues underpinning the capitalist system and the psychology of human behaviors.

Back then, I knew a little about money. However, I saw the consequences of financial poverty: limited access to economic opportunities and lack of freedom to pursue one's life passions. Everyday life seemed full of uncertainty and was a constant struggle for survival. I could see how hard my parents worked and still they were unable to make ends meet. I remember being unable to hold a conversation about money at the family dinner table for fear of arousing negative emotions. Deep in my heart, I promised myself that someday I would be rich and take care of my parents and family.

I was born in Buhera, Zimbabwe, over three decades ago to two wonderful parents. My mother was a dedicated stay-at-home spouse and farmer. My dad worked for a tobacco processing company in Harare, the capital of Zimbabwe. Needless to say, I spent most of my childhood in Buhera. As the firstborn in a family of three kids, I grew up herding cattle, like most children of my age group in my native Zimbabwe. Life was far removed from the realities of the busy capitalistic world—no stock market, no hustle and bustle of city life, no paying for rent and utilities. Most of our food and livelihood revolved around communal subsistence farming. We grew most of our own food, hunted for game meat in the neighboring forests, and sometimes kept home-grown chickens.

Summertime in Buhera was characterized by beautiful weather and mostly clear blue skies, along with a warm breeze that was present for much of the year. The winters were cold but not even close to the freezing weather I have experienced in Canada. My first experience with snow occurred in December 2014, after I immigrated to Canada. Since for most of my childhood I enjoyed a very warm climate, I appreciated the sunny days in Canada, particularly after the brutal chilly weather characteristic of Canadian winters. I enjoy walking in the summer, when I meet Canadians who are quick to strike up a conversation and talk about how beautiful the weather is – and a multitude of other topics, including personal finance. This is something I very much cherish in my new country.

In addition, I fondly remember how peaceful the Buhera community was. Also, the community had a robust support system of aunties and uncles. In Zimbabwean culture, there is a common adage that it takes the whole village to raise a child. For example, if one villager observes a child from the same community doing something wrong, the villager may go directly to the child's parents and report the misbehavior. This unity of purpose and mutual responsibility of the community fostered a sense of love and a healthy support system.

Buhera village had a population of 271,920[1] in 2023, mostly living in sparsely spaced houses. The community is also endowed with rich nature, rivers, and vegetation. The atmosphere is often punctuated by birds chirping, contributing to a serene ecosystem. In summer, we would go and bathe in the free-flowing water of the Nyazvidzi river before

---

[1] https://www.citypopulation.de/en/zimbabwe/admin/manicaland/101__buhera/ Accessed online on December 31, 2023.

going to look for our cattle close to sunset. The cattle are released from their pens in summer mornings to graze in the communal lands with no supervision, before being locked back in their pens close to sunset.

Despite the modest background of my upbringing, I was fortunate to have parents who valued education. My parents encouraged me to work hard in school as they believed that education is an essential life skill. I remember my dad coming home with newspapers and books he thought would help me understand what was happening around the world. Consequently, I remember reading a lot of material about the politics in Africa. A few that come to mind now include issues around the civil war that was raging in the Democratic Republic of Congo (DRC). The DRC is an African country considered to be the richest nation globally in terms of unextracted mineral wealth. Sadly, in the DRC, most of the population lives on less than a dollar a day. The good news is that an end to the civil war in 1996 brought peace to most parts of the country. The Southern African Development Community (SADC), of which my native Zimbabwe is a part, played an integral role in bringing back peace and stability to the DRC. The SADC is a regional body comprising 15 African states with a core mandate to achieve economic development, peace and security, growth, and regional integration.

Since my parents encouraged me to work hard in school, I found myself reading and enjoying books from an early age. I completed my primary and high school education in Buhera before proceeding to study at the University of Zimbabwe (UZ) in 2006. What fascinated me the most when I first moved to Harare to pursue my academic studies was the glitter and joy of city life. Harare is the capital city of Zimbabwe, popularly known as the sunshine city because of the abundant sunshine typically present throughout the year. The UZ is in the Mount Pleasant suburb, a quiet and affluent neighborhood of Harare.

My experiences at the UZ, where I read for a B.Sc. degree in economics, were wonderful. I affectionately remember taking a sequence of courses in the economics department, including microeconomics, macroeconomics, introduction to statistics, and international economics. What stood out the most about my economics courses was the concept of scarcity of resources. At UZ, I also had the chance to take elective courses in other departments, such as Introduction to Psychology. Little did I know that this course would help me appreciate the behavioral aspects of people in the world of investing.

Fast forward to 2010. Upon completing my B.Sc., I could not find gainful employment in Zimbabwe. At that time, five per cent of the university graduates across the country were unemployed and in 2023, eight per cent of recent graduates remain unemployed.[2] Consequently, I was a statistic of unemployment in Zimbabwe. It was disappointing, but rather than blaming and looking for someone to blame and focusing on the negative, I decided instead to volunteer most of my time with local non-profits. However, I remained resolute in my desire to further my education. I applied for every scholarship I could find online that was aligned with my academic interests. I had developed a special interest in agricultural and resource economics.

After four years of applying for scholarships abroad, I was eventually awarded the Mastercard Foundation Scholarship to read for a Master of Food and Resources in Economics (MFRE) at the University of British Columbia (UBC), Canada. This opportunity changed my life for good. For the first time in my life, I would eventually leave my native Zimbabwe to start a new life far away from my family. Even from my days as a boy in Buhera village, the idea of studying abroad had captured my imagination. I recall during the early days of my childhood herding cattle with my friends, chasing after airplanes each time they passed above us. It was so much fun and a rewarding exercise!

I landed in Vancouver, Canada in July 2014. The experience was phenomenal. I was unsure whether to celebrate or cry with joy upon landing at Vancouver International Airport. My now close friend, Kuzivakwashe (Kuzi) Mutonga, whom I had met previously in Zimbabwe, was also studying at UBC. Kuzi had shared the Mastercard Foundation

---

[2]https://www.macrotrends.net/countries/ZWE/zimbabwe/unemployment-rate. Caution must be taken with this data. Zimbabwe has a large number of its working population working in the informal sector since they could not find formal employment.

Scholars Program with me as he thought that I would be a good fit for the program. Essentially, the Mastercard Foundation Scholarship program started off as a $500 million initiative that was dedicated to educating the next generation of African leaders from poor economic backgrounds. The foundation has since increased funding for scholarships both in Africa and partner universities around the world. Kuzi had brought along with him Brian Mukweswe, a remarkable young man who was studying engineering at UBC and is also now a close friend. Like me, Brian came from a similarly poor background, in Uganda. It was such a pleasure to meet these two young men as they would help me navigate Vancouver, showing me the best places to visit and eat out and other essentials.

I graduated at UBC with the MFRE degree in 2015, with the honor of being selected as valedictorian by the dean of the Land and Food Systems department. What fascinated me most about the MFRE program was its applied nature. I remember taking a course in commodity trading where we used fake money to trade commodities such as wheat in real time via the Chicago Mercantile Exchange (CME). This course was a revelation for me in my wealth-building journey as it offered me a glimpse of how the stock market functioned. Post-UBC graduation, I began freelance consulting for two UBC professors. I learned a great deal about drafting technical reports, handling huge data sets, and applying them to solve real-world problems.

A few years later, this consulting opportunity led me to an offer to work as a research assistant within UBC's Institute for the Oceans and Fisheries. I started the Ph.D. program in 2018, before eventually transferring into an M.A. program in Resources, Environment and Sustainability. Two years into the Ph.D. program, I realized that it was not the right time, nor a good fit for me, and that led me to transfer into an M.A. program after successfully completing my Ph.D. coursework. I was lucky to have an incredibly supportive supervisor, Dr. Rashid Sumaila. I remember having a conversation with him while walking to the UBC bus loop. He advised me to take the time to reflect on what I really wanted to do in life and do it well. I completed the M.A. in May 2021 and felt it was time for me to explore the real world. I was super excited about the prospect of facing new challenges outside of the ivory tower of academia. I looked forward to being on the streets of life without the protective bubble university sometimes provided.

During the decade I have lived in Canada, I have been fascinated with the idea of building wealth. However, I did not really have anyone to teach me how to do it. Over the years, I have made many investment mistakes, and I am certain to make more mistakes in the future—and that is a part of the wealth-building journey.

After completing my M.A., I started to think more about future financial wellbeing. I am fortunate to live in Canada, which has great social support systems including our healthcare system, better job prospects, and a stable environment for entrepreneurs. In writing this book, I thought of the benefits of creating a digital imprint in the form of a book that documents my wealth-building experiences.

In addition, I thought my life experiences as a student of personal finance and investing might inspire a wider audience—and not merely my own children. Coming from a Zimbabwean culture where most of my elders had life wisdom and yet did not always document it, I sought to break this cycle. More than anything else, I also felt obligated to share my experiences on this journey that I will call, *the* intelligent millennial investor. This evolved from my profound respect for the wisdom I gained from the seminal book by Benjamin Graham, *the intelligent investor*. This book is so profound that, despite first being published in 1949, most of its contents are still applicable in the investment landscape today. I thought that perhaps if I authored a book, and left it in our home library, our children might learn a few things from my past experiences. Even better if they avoid the mistakes I have made in this wealth-building journey.

Most of the examples and analysis in this book are based on my lived experiences in both Zimbabwe and Canada. I will also share some experiences I have gained through reading a wide range of books and through my academic background as a trained economist. Most importantly, I will also share my experiences as a practicing student of personal finance and a retail investor in the United States and Canadian stock exchanges. I have learned that, just as if one wants to lose weight, the intention alone will not automatically produce the intended result. However, results will come from the compounding of good habits such as consistently working out, maintaining a healthy diet, and consuming less sugar. And so it is with personal finance and investing. My research and experience persuade me to believe that while it is important to read widely, building wealth involves a blend of research, hard work and practicing some of the basic principles I will outline over the next nine chapters. At the end of the book, I will share some of the books that have been foundational and informative in my personal wealth-building journey. The goal of wealth is to leave a legacy for the long term. I hope these experiences will provide some perspective on the important matters of wealth building.

In this book, in this chapter, I offer an introduction to the readers. Then in chapter 2, I outline steps I consider to be foundational to improve one's odds of becoming wealthy and living a happy and fulfilled life throughout this journey. This includes having a specific *education* in a particular field. This education, if applied optimally, can potentially provide a cutting-edge advantage in terms of higher earnings and a better understanding of one's area of specialty. This can be leveraged to personal finance and investing as I will explain in the coming chapters.

Secondly, but still under chapter 2, I share the importance of understanding how money works. Then in chapter 3, I share my thoughts and experiences on the *impact of debt* that can be helpful in accelerating the wealth-building goal. In chapter 4, I outline the importance of having *savings* in a household, particularly an emergency fund. Then explain how an individual can cushion themselves against emergencies and leverage their savings to their investment portfolio. This would be even better for wealth building if one takes advantage of the compounding effect of starting early.

In chapter 5, I introduce the concept of the *stock market*, focusing on the most basics that have helped me to get started investing in the United States and Canadian stock exchanges. Also, past evidence in personal finance development shows that shortcuts to building wealth often result in catastrophic consequences. So far, I am learning that taking a long-term anchored approach can be beneficial in allowing the money to compound over time, while not assuming too much risk in the securities I invest in.

To offer readers my thought process on *how to pick stocks* or securities to invest in. So, I devote chapter 6 to explain the criteria that I apply when I invest. I frequently hear stories of people who lost the fortune they worked so hard to build because of speculating, all in a quest to get rich faster. The more I started reading and learning about investing, the more I started appreciating the importance of patience in building wealth. I also devote a section to the concept of compounding interest in investing. Compound interest is a powerful concept in other areas of life as well, such as relationships, building businesses, and exercising. I provide simple examples to illustrate the power of compound interest and illustrate the rule of 72.

Chapter 7, I focus on how diversification of assets is important to successful investing before turning to offer insights on *estate planning* in the last chapter.

Chapter 2: The Essence of Specific Education in Building Wealth

*"Income = Accountability + Leverage + **Specific Knowledge**" Eric Jorgenson*

In 2020, I came to the realization that I had spent most of my life *dreaming* about financial freedom but not actually taking concrete steps to achieve it, other than acquiring degrees. Fortunately, as I later realized, economics provided me with a better understanding of basic personal finance and investing concepts. I consider understanding the power of compound interest and understanding how global financial systems work to be particularly important to personal finance. When it hit me, I sat down and started to self-introspect about a time-bound path to building wealth and defining what it takes to live a happy and fulfilled life.

The first step I took was to immediately, purposefully educate myself on personal finance through research and study, reading many finance-related books and watching educational material on YouTube. I also started connecting some of the life and academic education I had acquired over the years. This was my first step in acquiring *specific knowledge* of wealth building. As I started reading the basics of finance and investments in general, I faced an obvious challenge. There are too many personal finance and investing resources available online. Hence, given the amount of available online resources, I needed to develop a systematic way to synthesize relevant material in the least possible time. I realized early on that I needed a remarkably simple strategy if I were to succeed in acquiring wealth-building soft skills.

The second thing my partner and I did was to think of *how much* money we would need to become financially independent. Financial independence meant a point where we could live off our passive income and without the need to work to earn money to cater to our basic living expenses. Thirdly, we also needed to have an appreciation of *how long* it might take to hit the retirement target—the *Financial Freedom* number as I will call it in this book.

I must admit that this was not an easy mental assignment. However, with the help of my partner, I sat down and started off by just asking ourselves how much we were currently spending on basic living expenses and then started imagining, in simple terms, how much we would need if we were to retire today—barring unforeseen circumstances.

Removing unknowns such as potential future income changes, inflation rates etc. I also deliberately decided to focus on the private pension plan where we would retire on income from our own investments. The pension system is one of the main government-sponsored sources of income for most retirees in Canada[3]. It has three tiers that include the Canada Pension Plan (CPP) for the rest of Canada and Quebec Pension Plan (QPP) for those who live in Quebec, the Old Age Security (OAS) and the private pension plans that include income from private sources such as inheritances and investments in registered accounts such as Tax-Free Savings Account, and home equity, etc.

a) Canada Pension Plan

The CPP is funded by the contributions of employees, employers, and self-employed individuals, as well as the revenue earned on CPP investments. Some key considerations about the CPP include:

1. Canada Pension Plan Retirement Pension: The CPP retirement pension provides income to individuals who have made contributions to the CPP and are at least 60 years old[4]. The amount of the retirement pension is based on how much an individual has contributed and how long they have been making contributions to the CPP;

---

[3]https://www.investopedia.com/terms/c/cpp.asp.
[4] https://www.canada.ca/en/services/benefits/publicpensions.html.

2. Canada Pension Plan Disability Benefits: The CPP disability benefits are available to individuals who are unable to work due to a disability[5];

3. Benefits for Canadians Abroad: The CPP also provides benefits for Canadians who live outside of Canada.

b) Old Age Security Pension

The OAS pension is a monthly payment available to individuals who are 65 years of age or older and have lived in Canada for at least 10 years, even if they have never worked[6].

1. Guaranteed Income Supplement: The Guaranteed Income Supplement (GIS) is a benefit that low-income OAS recipients may be eligible to receive;

2. Allowance for people aged 60 to 64: The Allowance is a benefit available to the spouses or common-law partners of GIS recipients who are between the ages of 60 and 64[7].

Since I plan to work and contribute to the Canadian pension system, the income I will receive when I become financially free will be extra income but for the purpose of this book, I focus on my own retirement plan so that I can control the withdrawal rate or income I will contribute over the next couple of years. I also considered a conservative approach that inflation rate would be an average of two percent in the United States (U.S) and Canada where I invest most of my money and assume the return on asset prices in the US as five per cent[8] annually.

However, recently, inflation has been quite high both in the US and Canada. Hence, my realistic real rate of return net of inflation I would expect to get over the next couple of years would be about 5%/year. Based on the December data, the reported inflation in the US for the year 2023 as reported in January 2024 was 3.4%[9]. What this means is that, in

[5] https://www.canada.ca/en/services/benefits/publicpensions.html.
[6] https://www.canada.ca/en/services/benefits/publicpensions.html.
[7]https://www.canada.ca/en/services/benefits/publicpensions.html.
[8]https://www.macrotrends.net/2526/sp-500-historical-annual-returns.
[9] https://www.usinflationcalculator.com/inflation/current-inflation-rates/

my investing strategy, I have to factor in the inflation of above the 2% target over the next couple of years.

If my investments give me a higher return than the Standard & Poor's (SPX) benchmark, then that could help, but historically, it is a challenging feat to beat this index. Another approach is to work more years than I expect or immigrate to a country with a lower cost of living. However, this may come with some potential risks of a poor healthcare system and a lower quality of life for me and my family, compared to staying in Canada.

Over the past 98 years, the SPX has returned an average of eight percent per year since 1928. The SPX is a popular benchmark that is used to track market performance in the United States by most investors. More about this later in chapter five.

In my quest to find resources on how to estimate the amount we will need to financially retire; I found a book that resolved my understanding of our retirement income needs. That book is *Quit Like a Millionaire* by Kristy Shen and Bryce Leung. I deliberately mention that it is financially free, and not retirement because it is important to work and find something meaningful, even though we will not be working for money.

For me, the major takeaway from the book was the formula for calculating the desired retirement income target. Simply put, the formula estimates the desired future income I would need to be financially free. For example, if I want to be financially free, on a monthly income of $4,000 adjusted for inflation to cover my family living expenses. To calculate my financial freedom number, I simply multiply the monthly living expenses number by 12 to determine annual expenses. Then multiply the annual expenses by a factor of 25 (e.g., $4,000 x 12 x 25 = $1,200,000).[10]

So, my hypothetical Financial Freedom number for retirement income in this example would be $1.2 million after tax. This methodology is based on studies that were done by researchers who ran a series of scenarios using the Monte Carlo simulations to establish

---

[10]The money is in Canadian dollars adjusted for inflation.

the optimal withdrawal rate retirees could withdraw for a minimum of thirty years without exhausting their money before they die[11]. I also ignore other potential retirement income streams in the Canadian context, such as CPP and the OAS in my estimation, as I indicated in the preceding paragraphs. I share the mathematics behind the formula later in the appendix section of the book.

Obviously, the two questions that then occupy my financial freedom journey are, how am I going to raise that amount, and how long would it take to hit that target retirement income level? So, hang on and I will answer those questions in the next chapters.

Creating a Financial Plan: Create a Budget

As a student of personal finance, I was surprised by how uncomfortable it was for me to craft a personal budget, notwithstanding the obvious importance of developing a financial plan. One of the highlights of my academic journey includes the lessons from my time as an economics student at the UZ. The main takeaway from the macroeconomics course was understanding fiscal policy; pretty much how the government receives revenues and spends it. As an example, and without going into too much detail, the Canadian economy consists of small units (micro units) such as individuals who *consume* goods and services, and businesses such as banks and retail shops that *provide* goods and services to people. When the activities of all these highlighted players are added together, the impact to the economy becomes macroeconomic (bigger) scale.

Now, simplifying this to an individual level, one of the things I found to be elusive to most people, based on conversations with many friends and colleagues, is the concept of a budget—in simple terms, a statement of income and expenses over a defined period, perhaps just a month. I recall feeling uncomfortable while chequing my bank account balance on my mobile bank app; I feared the reality that I was likely overspending. Fortunately, I finally decided that enough was enough and was ready to take a turn on

---

[11]Blanchett, D. (2023). Redefining the Optimal Retirement Income Strategy. *Financial Analysts Journal, 79*(1), 5-16.

my financial independence journey. I started off by developing an Excel spreadsheet listing all my expenses and income streams.

With the advent of technology, there are a few apps that can be used to track expenses when linked to bank accounts. I am however quite sensitive to my privacy and uncomfortable with the idea of giving away my spending patterns to a third party. Hence, I prefer the old way of using an excel spreadsheet that lists all my incurred expenses and incomes. Also, there are numerous online templates that have formulas; one can download these templates and input expenses and income. What I found profound when I started doing my own budget and constantly tracking my expenses is an unusual pattern of some runaway expenses that unexpectedly claim a fair portion of my income. These include dining out, online shopping, and online subscriptions. While my family and I enjoy going out and restaurant meals, we try to stick to our budget.

Another important lesson that has emerged from me tracking my monthly budget was that I immediately noticed areas where we were overspending. I used to pay subscription fees for unlimited TV channels, when in fact most news in today's era can be livestreamed. I also noted that I was paying a large monthly phone bill. However, since most of the time I work from home and have internet access, I decided to cut off these unnecessary expenses. In a nutshell, cutting out some of the luxuries immediately freed up some money to put towards savings.

When crafting a budget, I have learnt that it is important to be realistic and honest about one's income and expenditures. While it is good to be ambitious, I consider it crucial to also live and enjoy life and not become fixated on destination arrival. Retirement is a relative concept. Hence, I believe in the need to strike a balance between spending in the present and in the future. Now, let us turn to creating a budget. A budget can help provide perspective on one's financial situation.

Things to consider when creating a budget

Be honest about your current financial situation throughout the budget creating process. In terms of income, I think of my current income streams such as day job, side hustle, spousal income if they are working and freelancing income etc.

In terms of expenses, I like to think of the fundamental things that I will need for services, and I list all those on the table below. I then consider some expenses I do for fun and the money I have to set aside for future activities. The big purchases for me may include items such as money set aside for vacation and buying a house. I also consider personal development expenses as online courses. In my case, in 2024, I paid for an online course for trading.

Table 2. Framework for building a budget

Fundamentals	Fun	Future Expenses	Retirement Portfolio
Mortgage/rent	Clothing	Emergency fund	Equities, treasury bills
Transportation	Drinks	Extra debt payments	Rental income
Insurance	Eating out	Self-development	Bonds, Cash in highly liquid accounts
Groceries	Donations	Education fund, vacation fund	
Healthcare	Subscriptions such as Netflix & Amazon prime	House fund	

Simple exercise

1. List all your income and expenses in a simple excel spreadsheet.
2. Income includes your paycheck and all money from side hustles, dividends from investments if you have any etc.
3. List expenses such as phone bills, rent/mortgages, etc.
4. Savings and investment (income minus all expenses).

On average, millionaires have multiple streams of income from various sources, not a single income stream. The income streams may include employment or business income, investments in the stock market in stocks, bonds, fixed income security, real estate, gold, etc. For most people, living expenses may include rent/mortgage, phone bills and food. So, as a millennial building their wealth, the key is to work towards starting to invest in the stock market and get into real estate earlier, if possible. The most important thing is to be educated first on how to invest in the stock market and other investment securities, because investing comes with risks, especially one that is not a professional in the investing landscape. In the next chapter, I share my insights on debt, so fasten your seatbelts!

Chapter 3: Understanding debt

"The borrower is servant to the lender" Proverbs 22.7

Over the years, I have done my best to avoid getting into debt by borrowing money. In North America, it is quite easy to access a line of credit, which is a form of debt. There are many reasons why people may get into debt. These may include borrowing to buy a house or car, paying for an education through education loans, or even using margin accounts to invest in the stock market.

Investopedia defines a margin account as a brokerage account in which a trader's broker-dealer lends them cash to purchase stocks or other financial products and hold the securities within the account as collateral to the loan. This is quite risky especially if one loses the borrowed money. I have read stories of people online who borrowed money and invested in the stock market when there was a positive sentiment and lost it all when the market dropped. What this means is that they borrow money to invest, and if they lose it all, it will have to be repaid back, regardless of the loss. This is a double tragedy that I have learnt to avoid. However, oftentimes the untold story reveals how many of these borrowers struggle with debt and interest on their loans as a result of the quest to become rich quickly.

Statistics on the level of indebtedness in Canada and the United States are shocking. In December 2020, the household debt ratio for Canadians rose to 170.7 percent, up from 162.8 per cent in the second quarter according to Statistics Canada. In other words, Canadians owed an average of $1.71 for every dollar of their disposable income[12]. Hence, the intelligent millennial investor needs to be careful when dealing with debt. As noted above, in some cases people take on debt overconfident that they will pay it off sooner

---

[12]https://www.bnnbloomberg.ca/household-debt-ratio-rises-to-170-7-per-cent-statcan-says-1.1535105.

rather than later. However, statistics on the level of debt indicate otherwise. Therefore, debt needs to be handled with due care; it can be a double-edged sword that can help build wealth or destroy the borrower's ability to achieve financial independence.

On the positive side, when utilized carefully, debt can accelerate wealth-building. My first experience with debt in Canada occurred in 2014 when I landed in the country to pursue my studies at UBC. When the school term began in the first week of September, the Big Five Canadian banks (Toronto Dominion Bank, Bank of Nova Scotia, Canadian Imperial Bank of Commerce, Bank of Montreal, and Royal Bank of Canada) set up booths on the UBC campus. Their goal was to market their financial products, including bank accounts and credit cards to students. When I immigrated to Canada in 2014, I opened my first bank account with one of the top Canadian banks. Not long after I opened my bank account, I received my first credit card offer in my mailbox, with a credit limit of $500. I remember not even using that credit card until a year later, after I graduated. Fortunately, given my prior experience living in Zimbabwe where there was limited access to credit cards, I have been very cautious enough to pay it off after every purchase.

One such salient insight is that people tend to be generally *overconfident* in their abilities to build wealth quickly and yet *underestimate* risks associated with the process. To successfully build wealth, first and foremost the Intelligent Millennial Investor should learn how to use debt skillfully to their advantage.

1. Mortgage

Mortgage is the loan that is extended to borrowers for the purposes of buying a house. In 2020 alone, Canadians added $118 billion in mortgage and car debt to hit a total of $2 trillion[13]. As of 2022, more than a third[14] Canadians own a home with half of this on variable interest. However, there has been an increasing number of Canadians struggling

---

[13]Canadians now owe more than $2 trillion, Equifax says | CBC News
[14]https://www.canada.ca/en/financial-consumer-agency/programs/research/financial-well-being-mortgages.html.

to pay off their debts due to the increasing cost of living both in Canada and the US. Of those who have mortgages, seventy per cent[15]are estimated by the Bank of Canada to be on a fixed interest rate. The thirty per cent who are on variable interest rate mortgages will see their payments increase over the next couple of years.

The Investopedia defines a fixed interest as an unchanging rate charged on a liability, such as a loan or a mortgage. Conversely, a variable interest rate refers to the interest rate that is levied on a liability that changes over time. As an example, if one gets a mortgage in Canada which usually has an amortization of say, 25 years broken down into five terms of five-year periods. If the bank of Canada increases their policy rates, the banks which may have loaned clients mortgage on variable interest rate may see their mortgage payments increasing as well. This can happen if the BoC was to reduce the policy rates.

The Investopedia defines amortization as a period in which a debt such as a mortgage is reduced or paid off by regular payments. In Canada, mortgages are typically split into 5-year terms and the mortgage payments can be either paid either bi-weekly or monthly.

It is common practice in Canada for borrowers for mortgage loans to refinance their mortgages after five years if the home equity has increased. What this means is the borrowers may renegotiate their existing mortgage loan agreement[16]or use equity in the property to increase the mortgage loan amount and finance purchase of a bigger property.

It is common practice for mortgage borrowers to pay higher insurance when they get a mortgage loan if they do not have at least 20 percent of the total property value. Insurance covers the potential risk premium if they default in mortgage loan payments in the future.

---

[15] https://www.bankofcanada.ca/2022/06/opening-statement-090622/.
[16] http://tinyurl.com/mortgageloan2024.

Many people obtained mortgages in 2020 due to the low rates from lenders which were related to the BoC rates which had been reduced to prop up consumer spending after the COVID-19 pandemic hit. However, when the BoC started raising interest rates to curb rising inflation rates in June 2022, some mortgage holders were left vulnerable due to increased payments on variable interest holders.

Fig 3.1. The graph below shows the overnight lending rates in Canada (1992-2023)

Source: Tradingeconomics.com and Bank of Canada

Most people assume that a mortgage is an acceptable risk, as it is the type of debt that has been shown to historically generate some positive returns in Canada and the US as the value of the equity increases as the property price rises overtime. If history is anything to go by regarding policy interest rates changes, it can be tricky having a variable interest rate mortgage in a high interest rate environment. Policy interest rates can rise fast depending on the changing macroeconomic environment. Fig 3.1 shows that in the early 1990s, the policy rates were quite high, compared to how they have increased over the past three decades. Fig. 3.1 depicts that, from the low interest rates environment of 2020, the Bank of Canada has been increasing interest rates quickly since 2022, up from near zero rates to about 5% by the end of 2023.

Thus, for most millennials of my age, it is important to get a mortgage loan, but to also understand the differences between a fixed and a variable interest mortgage as I have explained in the preceding chapter. I remember first hearing about this high interest rate environment when I was having dinner with one of my mentors. He cautioned me whether I fully understood that mortgage interest rates can go on the high end especially if the BoC tried to contain inflation.

In Canada, real estate has been going up for the past decade. However, like every other security, it is not always true that real estate prices are ever-increasing. Fig 3.2 demonstrates that there were other years, such as between 2022 and 2023, where there were declines in home prices.

Fig 3.2. Canada real estate market trends

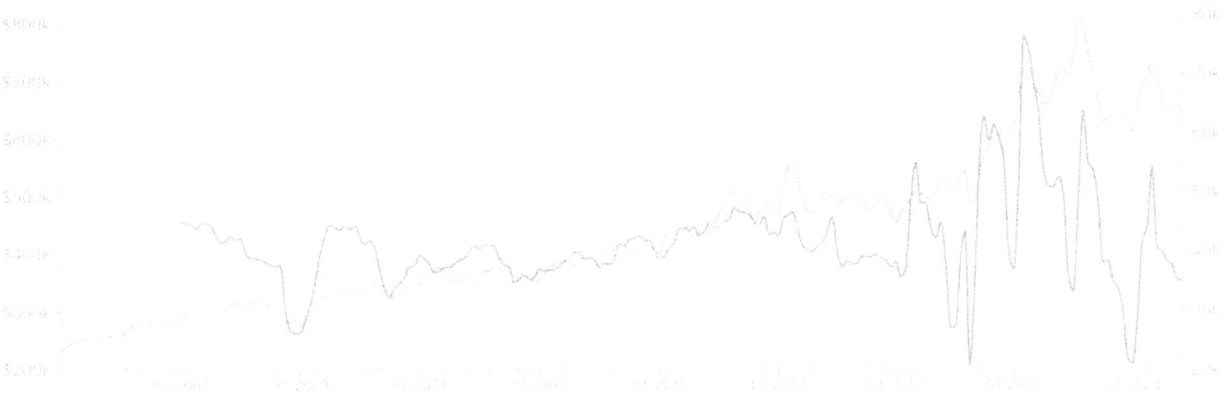

Source: https://wowa.ca/reports/canada-housing-market.

On the graph, the orange line shows the average sold price of houses over time and the blue line indicates the seasonally adjusted transactions in the real estate market.

However, the graph shows that in Canada, the real estate prices have had a general upward trend over the long term. The takeaway for me from this trend is that, when I decide to get into a mortgage, I should get in with the intention to keep the house for a long term, to avoid paying high transaction costs e.g. real estate agent fees.

It is also important to be aware that owning a house can pose challenges if one decides to relocate across Canada or to other parts of the world. Of course, one may rent out the house for a fee, but there might be potential risks, such as the renter not paying the rent some months or maintenance costs of the house. Of course, history cannot be a definite indicator for the future, but it at least gives me some perspective on one of the most important decisions of my life.

As with any form of debt, the intelligent millennial investor should be careful with mortgage debt. A general rule of thumb I use is to make sure one has at least 6–12 months' worth of savings in a highly liquid account, such as a chequing account. Then one can raise the down payment, which starts at five percent of the total value of the property for first home buyers. In this case, it may be helpful to buy mortgage insurance which costs extra on top of the mortgage when you have a smaller down payment. Also, the higher the down payment, the lower the mortgage monthly repayments, as the risk profile falls with the homebuyer paying more up front. In Canada, the down payment varies depending on the value of the property the individual wants to buy. In Table 3.1, below, I provide some information as set out by the Financial Consumer Agency of Canada on the minimum down payment needed to buy a house.

In addition, the federal government in Canada has come up with initiatives to support first home buyers plans. I will talk more about this in chapter 4 under various ways to optimize taxes. But, in a nutshell, the home buyer's plan[17] is a federal program that allows eligible Canadians to withdraw money from their retirement savings plans (RRSPs) to buy or build a qualifying home. If a prospective home buyer has 20% worth of money to pay for a down payment for a house, it can help waive the house insurance fees which can be quite substantial.

____

[17] https://www.canada.ca/en/revenue-agency/services/tax/individuals/topics/rrsps-related-plans/what-home-buyers-plan.html.

Table 3.1: The minimum down payment on home purchases in Canada

Home purchase price	Minimum down payment
$500,0000 or less	5% of the purchase price.
$500,00,000 -$999,999	5% of the first $500k of the purchase price. 10% for the portion of the purchase price above $500,000.
$1 million or more	20% of the purchase price.

Source: Financial Consumer Agency of Canada

Many people I have spoken to within my friendship circles generally rush into mortgages and then later find themselves in situations where they are house poor. This is a situation whereby one may not have the ability to have any extra savings or money outside of the equity locked up in the mortgage such that even if there is a maintenance request, they may end up borrowing from the bank. Generally, when buying a house, the associated costs include closing costs, furnishing, maintenance, and property taxes that are levied yearly after buying a house. If one does not run their numbers well and make sure they have a decent financial cushion by way of an emergency fund or other easily liquid financial securities, rushing into a mortgage can potentially prove quite stressful. Significant real estate debt can also be a burden, especially when there is an economic shock such as the market corrections that happened in 2009 and March 2020.

Starting mid-2022, because of the rising inflation rates in Canada, the Bank of Canada increased interest rates and those who had variable interest rates mortgages found themselves paying more money for their mortgages. The intelligent millennial investor should be careful to invest in securities they fully understand rather than rushing in because of Fear of Missing Out (FOMO). Therefore, one should do some research on the property they intend to purchase and raise the largest down payment possible before even considering buying a property.

Many people argue that it is always a good idea to buy a home because one must live somewhere, and if one does not own a home, one still has to pay rent. This is so because getting a mortgage loan for a house may come with maintenance and other associated costs such as agent fees, lawyer fees to transfer the property to the new owner. However, it is also true that no one can possibly care more about your investments than you do. And over-leveraging with debt is not a good idea for anyone, especially the conservative investor. As Warren Buffet has remarked on more than one occasion, "You only learn who has been swimming naked when the tide goes out,"[18] as we saw in 2020 when the COVID-19 pandemic hit and with the changing interest rates environment due to evolving monetary policies by central bankers around the world. Those who can keep cash in hand can also take advantage during housing market corrections when most overleveraged homebuyers crash, and the banks come after them.

While talking to realtors may help provide some perspective on the housing market, it is like asking a barber if one needs a haircut. Most realtors earn their living through commissions, so they tend to be salespeople and push their own interests. It is business. The bottom line is to amass a sizable deposit and a portion of the closing costs before considering a real estate purchase.

While home ownership may seem easy, it is also one area where FOMO can drive people to the brink of crippling debt. I have had conversations with colleagues and friends who rushed into buying homes and later realized that they were not financially ready to buy a home. However, at that point they are already locked into home ownership contracts. A case in point is the realtor in Ontario, Canada, who got hit with a mortgage penalty fine of $30,000 after she was forced to sell her home following her inability to pay the mortgage during COVID-19.[19] These stories of ordinary people who suddenly find themselves in debt are not often published—yet doing so would help spread awareness to potential

---

[18]https://www.berkshirehathaway.com/letters/2007ltr.pdf.
[19]https://www.cbc.ca/news/business/mortgage-penalty-pandemic-1.5588741.

young buyers. Getting out of a mortgage before its term expires can result in a financial penalty.

Another point worth noting is the issue of buying a house where one can afford to pay for the mortgage. Primary residence does generate a lot of tax benefits as there is no tax on capital gains when it is sold.

However, the intelligent millennial investor should be cautious when getting a house mortgage because too often people buy big houses they do not really need, incurring a large debt. House mortgage comes with interest payments over and above the principal loan. Consequently, some end up working multiple jobs just to stay afloat and continue with their inflated lifestyle. It is worth considering just what value a big home brings if the purchaser then spends most of their time outside of the house working to service the mortgage.

2. Credit card debt

Credit card debt is a source of financial misery for many people in North America. And any discussion of credit card debt must include a discussion of compound interest. In addition, the availability of credit cards in North America tempts many people to use them as a fallback plan. However, credit cards come with high interest fees, often as high as twenty percent annually. Interest is either good or bad depending on whether one is on the receiving or paying end.

Compound interest is one of the most powerful tools for building wealth. However, as I will explain in the next chapters, it can be a double-edged sword, especially if it works against an individual, as can happen with credit card debt. An intelligent millennial investor should be careful of the impacts of credit card debt, including extremely high interest rates and fees. The way I look at credit card debt is I imagine if I was getting the same annual rate of return on my investments as I would be paying for the credit card. It gives me a sobering perspective, and of course, people can have different financial circumstances, but generally, where possible, credit card debt can be challenging to pay off once one falls behind in monthly payments. Alternatively, compound interest can be a helpful tool to build wealth if the intelligent millennial investor receives interest on investments, instead of paying it out to lenders.

In 2017, the Bank of Canada reported that 89 percent of adult Canadians had at least one credit card. When the COVID-19 pandemic hit, some people found themselves unemployed and, without a savings cushion, began racking up credit card debt. Studies by Statistics Canada estimate that millennials carry more credit card debt compared to the older generation because of their higher propensity to succumb to online shopping.

Over the years, I have heard horror stories about being trapped in debt from friends who have been swallowed by credit card debt. I remember one day I met a friend by the Skytrain and not long after I exchanged pleasantries, they started to narrate that they were drowning in debt. It was quite concerning to me that they would go through such a stressful financial situation. While I am not prescribing how people should spend their money, it is a fact that credit card debt can yield very high interest rates which can compound over time.

In addition, I have also learned that it is especially important to have a good credit score in North America. A good credit history is essential, for example, if you want to obtain access to cheaper loans to buy a car on a payment plan. Many car dealerships perform credit checks for would-be buyers to make sure that they have sound credit history.

In 2021, the credit bureau Equifax—an organization responsible for performing credit checks and providing credit scores—reported that Canadians owe over $2 trillion in debt, with household debt of about $2.3 trillion[20]. Below, I briefly explain the various types of debts in North America.

---

[20]htttps://www.cbc.ca/news/business/equifax-canada-debt-1.5822589.

3. Car debt

As the name suggests, this is a type of loan extended to people who want to buy cars on credit. Most Canadians have car debts which they pay off gradually in the form of monthly payments. What is important is to avoid being lured into debt traps by falling victim to high-end cars that are often advertised on TV and online. The adverts can be tempting, and it is easy to get carried away. However, the reality is that a car is a depreciating asset unless it is used for business purposes.

I recall one day listening to Dave Ramsey, an American talk show host with expertise in financial education and credit counseling. One caller with a monthly income of $2,000 had called in to solicit financial advice. The caller mentioned that he had obtained a car loan for US$20,000. I found it shocking that the car dealership had extended the car loan to the caller, given his level of income, and given the higher cost of living in North America. Dave Ramsey was not kind to the caller for making the financial decision to purchase a car on credit, given his low level of income. However, as I had to quickly learn in North America, business is business. Sometimes it does appear that the capitalist system is one of dog-eat-dog. And some salespeople do what they need to sell their products and receive their commissions, regardless of the financial consequences to the buyer.

4. Line of credit

A line of credit is usually extended to a customer, who may be an individual or a business, through a bank or other financial institution. Typically, the line of credit will allow the client to withdraw money up to the agreed limit at a certain rate of interest. Lines of credit have lower interest rates compared to credit cards and are often secured (typically secured on a house). The interest rate is charged on the actual amount that is withdrawn by the customer.

Debt, as I have highlighted above, can take different forms. However, it can potentially stifle one's ability to save and ultimately invest and get an above inflation return in different securities. In simple terms, at an individual level debt means borrowing into the future, and that implies that money will need to be taken away from future earnings to pay off debt. However, as previously noted, if the individual can invest the borrowed money at a higher rate of return than the cost of the capital plus rate of inflation, it would make sense to borrow. The problem, as I will explain in Chapter 5 on the psychology of investing, is that human beings generally overestimate their intelligence in investing and underestimate the risks they assume.

5. Student debt situation in Canada

Student debt in Canada is an important topic for discussion as the cost of pursuing higher education has risen over the years. The national post newspaper reported that the latest annual data from Statistics Canada on tuition fees shows that the average yearly cost for Canadian undergraduates has increased to $7,076, up 2.9 per cent from the 2022-2023 academic year. In this regard, the amount of student debt outstanding in Canada is substantial, with Canada Student Loans (CSL) administering a portfolio of $18.2 billion in loans to over 1.7 million borrowers during the 2016/2017 school year[21].

Key highlights about student debt in Canada

1. Loan Disbursements: In the 2016/2017 academic year, Canada Student Loans disbursed $2.6 billion in loans to 490,401 students. Over the past ten years, CSL has disbursed 47% more in loans to 31% more students than in the previous decade[22].
2. Additional Financing: In addition to the federal government guaranteed loan program, graduates in Canada can also finance their studies through additional provincial student loans and private loans[23].
3. Student Debt Insolvencies: Student debt in Canada is considered a crisis, with negative consequences becoming increasingly evident. The number of

---

[21] https://www.hoyes.com/press/joe-debtor/the-student-debtor/
[22] https://www.hoyes.com/press/joe-debtor/the-student-debtor/.
[23] https://www.hoyes.com/press/joe-debtor/the-student-debtor/.

consumers insolvencies related to student debt, including personal bankruptcy and consumer proposals, is on the rise[24].

4. Average Debt at Graduation: Statistics on student debt in Canada, including the average debt at graduation, the percentage of graduates with large debt at graduation, and the percentage of graduates who have paid off their debt, vary by province and level of study[25].

5. Tax Deductions and Credits: There are various tax deductions and credits available for students in Canada, including deductions for moving expenses and childcare expenses, as well as non-refundable tax credits for tuition fees, books, public transit, and interest paid on student loans[26].

6. Repayment Period: If you have a Canada Student Loan, you will have a 6-month non-repayment period after finishing your final school term, reducing from full-time to part-time studies, or leaving school. This grace period allows borrowers time to transition before beginning loan repayment[27].

7. Debt Load: The debt load for students in Ontario is particularly high, with $2,301.5 million in student loans for both part-time and full-time students. Graduates in Alberta also face significant student loan debt[28].

Thoughts on debt management

Stuff happens in life. Consequently, it is not uncommon for people to find themselves in situations where borrowing high-interest-bearing loans may seem like the only available option, especially if they do not have an emergency fund. As noted earlier, when the return from borrowed capital is positive compared to the cost of serving the debt, it may make sense to carry debt. However, debt requires careful handling as the interest rate often becomes a burden when it gets out of control.

---

[24] https://www.hoyes.com/press/joe-debtor/the-student-debtor/.
[25] https://www150.statcan.gc.ca/t1/tbl1/en/tv.action?pid=371000360.
[26] https://www.canada.ca/en/financial-consumer-agency/services/pay-down-student-debt.html.
[27] https://www.canada.ca/en/financial-consumer-agency/services/pay-down-student-debt.html.
[28] https://www.consolidatedcreditcanada.ca/financial-news/student-loan-debt-forgiveness-in-canada/.

If one is in debt, depending on the circumstances such as the size and type of the debt, it is prudent to first and foremost acknowledge the situation. Acknowledging the debt situation may be a good idea before one even starts to clear off the debt. The next step would then be to produce a clear plan to pay it off as soon as possible, starting with whichever source of debt (i.e., credit card, car loan, etc.) has the highest interest rate.

I found some helpful information on how to deal with a debt situation on Innovation, Science and Economic Development Canada. This involves following a seven-step process as shown on the flow diagram below.

Six simple steps to freedom from debt

Step 1: Make a budget - as explained in Chapter 1, a budget is a crucial step in understanding the state of one's finances, by identifying the cash inflows and inflows at a given time.

Step 2: Check your credit health - credit score is a valuable tool that lenders use before lending to clients. Credit reports help show how creditworthy the client is, based on their history of paying bills on time. In Canada, the main credit agencies are TransUnion and Equifax. They offer credit scores ranging from 300 to 900, with 750[29] and above being considered excellent.

Step 3: Map out a plan - essentially, debt is the result when spending exceeds income. Ways to reduce debt may include reducing expenses, increasing cash flows, and paying off the outstanding amount owed. Once you know the full extent of your debt situation, it may be helpful to rank the debts in order of rate of interest. Financial experts recommend paying off the highest interest-yielding debt first as this results in reducing interest on debt, which is a cost to the debtor. This mathematically makes sense, but some people may be included to pay the smaller debts first regardless of the interest rate. This could

---

[29]http://www.ic.gc.ca/eic/site/icgc.nsf/eng/home.

potentially register some psychological 'victories' by clearing it off and giving an impetus to pay off the bigger amounts.

In extreme cases, debt counseling can help. There are many credit counseling companies across Canada and the US — just search the term online to find the nearest one. Credit counseling can help the debtor gain insights from an outsider and receive advice on paying off debt. These companies may also provide advice on how to deal with the psychological impact of the debt burden. This is significant because debt-related stresses can be profoundly painful and emotional.

Step 4: Take control and act - this stage may include actions such as starting to pay off the monthly installments for the debt as well as looking at alternatives such as debt bundling. The key here is to have a plan for paying it off and sticking to it until the debt is erased.

Step 5: Stretch your dollar - it is important to review your expenses to see potential money-saving areas. As noted earlier, one can make a budget and compare the needs versus the wants. Simple things like reevaluating online subscriptions and other luxuries one may be paying for may help unlock money to pay off debt. Other radical solutions can be as simple as reducing restaurant meals, using public transit, car-pooling with colleagues, finding a cheaper place to live, or finding cheaper house insurance.

Step 6: Planning ahead - once the debt repayment plan gets on track according to the budget, it is important to keep an eye on the future. While your budget will include amounts for savings and emergencies, you should always prepare for larger purchases, such as buying a car, household appliances, or even a new home. Plan and research these purchases before making a financial commitment. The goal is to avoid sliding back into debt, outside of an affordable home mortgage.

Moving forward - now that you have a budget, have identified cost saving areas, and have started paying off the debt, it is good to start thinking and planning for the long

term. This 6-step process outlined above provides a general pathway to improved financial security, but it is also important to consult financial or tax advisors.

Chapter 4: Building Savings

"Someone's sitting in the shade today because someone planted a tree a long time ago."
Warren Buffet

In this chapter, I will share my thoughts on how to build savings which I believe are important for one to cushion themselves from potentially borrowing high interest debt like payday loans. Building personal savings is an essential step towards financial security and achieving your financial goals. Over the past years Immigrated to Canada, I have learnt that having savings can be a great cushion. Not only because I am far away from most extended family members and also I have seen the benefits of having savings. As a retail investor, there are periods when the market presents opportunities to invest.

However, to achieve savings goals, it has been a deliberate process that requires discipline and dedication. Here are some tips that have helped me in building my personal savings:

1. Create a budget

Over the years, I have realized that having a budget is an important step to take control of my financial situation. As I have explained in chapter 2, when creating a budget, it is important to allocate a portion of your income towards savings.

2. Set savings goals.

Setting a savings goal is an important step because it can help to have a target and benchmark to track the progress or lack of it there. Each time I get income, I automatically set aside some of the money towards my savings. My savings target is at least 30% of every paycheck that I get. The key part also is to save up extra money that I unexpectedly earn from other side hustles rather than spending it all.

3. Build an emergency fund

My experience as a member of a low-income family in Zimbabwe was that every situation felt like an emergency because we had no savings to use for an inevitable rainy day. However, saving money requires discipline. Generally, most experts recommend an emergency fund of six–twelve months' worth of living expenses. I prefer having living expenses to last a year. Uncertainty and unexpected events may require one to activate the emergency fund as a backup financial reserve.

At some point in 2023, I had to rely on our family emergency fund when I was out of work. Unexpected events may include death of a family member or job loss, and this is when the emergency fund becomes handy. Death is unavoidable, but quite often I have seen people without life insurance or savings using the GoFundMe platform to cover funeral expenses. This can be avoided by building an emergency fund and having life insurance. There is nothing as stressful as having to deal with the loss of a loved one who may have been a breadwinner, and the potential loss of a home if you have a mortgage.

While there are many resources that provide free online education on how to build savings, I find Dave Ramsey's books and online resources particularly helpful. Dave Ramsey discourages individuals from borrowing money because chances are high that they will fail to pay it off in time. That is when in addition to the agreed interest, the interest may accrue even more on the principal loan. One only needs to listen to Ramsey's show to appreciate the degree of debt troubling people in North America.

A simple starting point is to have $1,000 in an emergency fund before starting to pay off the debt. Then once you pay off the debt, educate yourself about personal finance and build the emergency fund for 6–12 months' worth of living expenses. Once you have the optimal emergency fund set up, you can now start to invest for the long term.

The advantage of starting to invest after building an emergency fund is that the stock market often fluctuates and, in some cases, can go for three or so years in the negative. The most well-known negative period in the history of the S&P 500 Index, a popular benchmark used to track the market, was during the great depression. The S&P 500 ended the years between 1929 and 1932 in negative territory, with the worst performance being in 1931, when it dropped by 47.07 per cent. I will share more about the S&P 500 Index in chapter five. The red lines of the graphs indicate the years the S&P 500 closed down overall, and the green indicates when it closed the year in the positive territory. Please note that past performance does not guarantee future returns, so it is important to be cautious about basing one's decisions on the 'performance' descriptor. Investment returns also fluctuate overtime based on different market conditions such as investor sentiment which can be positive or negative.

Figure 4.1. A graph showing the performance of the S&P 500 between 1928- 2023

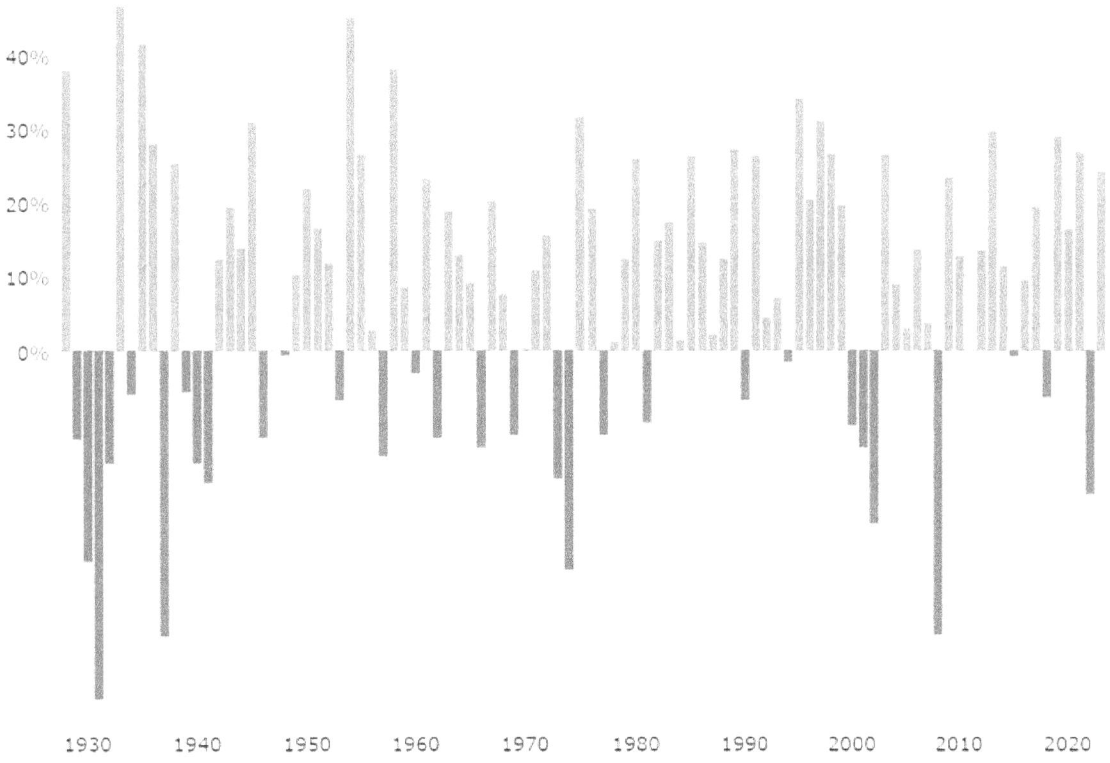

Source: www.macrotrends.net

As the late Charlie Munger, former trusted assistant of Warren Buffet said, the rule of thumb for compound interest is *she doesn't want to be interrupted.*" In other words, to be able to grow wealth through compound interest, one must be disciplined enough to invest over the long term. So, building an emergency fund enables one to have an opportunity to keep the invested money growing rather than liquidating the securities, even when they are down when there is financial need. More on investment strategies in the next chapters.

4. Determine your savings goals

Once the millennial investor builds an emergency fund they are comfortable with, next it is important to have clear savings goals to help motivate me towards savings. Whether the savings are for increasing an emergency fund to last longer in case of unexpected income fluctuations or other goals such as saving for a down payment on a house, saving towards a family vacation or planning for retirement. In my experience, having specific goals will give me a clear target to work towards.

5. Automate your savings

Once I determine that I want to save 30% of every paycheck, I then automate the transfer from my chequing account to various accounts. In my case, after I build an emergency fund for 6 months, my goal includes investing in the stock market for the long term. So, every time, I get back, I automate the money to be transferred into my different investment accounts for future allocation to different asset classes. Automating my savings has helped me achieve consistency in my goals as I no longer have to think about it. It has become a regular habit for me to save money towards my investment goals.

6. Reduce unnecessary expenses

After I automated my savings, I noticed that I now consistently review my spending habits and identify areas that need to be addressed. I also no longer worry about thinking about how much I should save and ultimately invest, because it is predetermined. If there is a change in my financial situation, then, I will adjust the savings automation accordingly. In some cases, I then consider cutting back on certain things like reducing discretionary expenses like dining out, entertainment, or subscriptions. Redirect the money saved towards your savings goals. This way I save loose change.

Another way I collect extra cash is by selling refundable drinks that we drink at home anyway. I deposit it into your savings account regularly. While it may seem small, over time, it can add up and contribute to your savings growth. My family also uses the similar approach by putting our living expenses on our credit cards and paying them off in full. This way, when done on credit cards with redeemable cash credit, on an annual basis, I usually cash out about $100. This can pay a few bills by taking advantage of the money that I would not have recovered. Caution should be on avoiding buying things on credit cards for the purpose of getting the cash refund. The idea is to use the cash refund on expenses I incur anyway.

7. Consider high-yield savings accounts

Recently, because of the fast growth of digital payment systems in all banks, most banks now offer online banking services. Digital banks offer an immediate advantage of no-fee chequing accounts. Examples of digital banks in Canada include the Equity bank and Tangerine. This could be a good place to keep an emergency fund only if they pay a positive interest rate because it can give a bit of an inflation cushion. Hence, once I build savings, I explore ways to keep the money in high-yield savings accounts that offer competitive interest rates. However, money for investment is allocated to investment accounts like I stated in the preceding paragraph.

8. Avoid high-interest debt

Once I build an emergency fund, I avoid high-interest debt, such as credit card debt, as it can hinder my ability to save and invest in investments that can yield high returns. Those with debt, it is important to focus on paying off debt while simultaneously building your savings.

9. Stay committed and explore other ways of increasing income streams

The process of building personal savings requires discipline and consistency. I stay committed to my savings goals and make saving a priority in my financial plan.

Remember, building personal savings takes time and effort. By implementing these tips and making saving a regular habit, you can make significant progress towards your financial goals.

10. Multiple streams of income

One of the ways that I look at building wealth is by simply adjusting the equation of my income versus the expenses. On one hand, I try to think of ways to increase my income streams while also not needlessly increasing our lifestyle. I also try to live my life and not be too frugal. The key for me and my family is to understand the things that we really need and those that are luxuries that we can postpone until we have higher income streams.

Having multiple streams of income is a key vehicle for building wealth. Millionaires usually have multiple streams of income from rental and dividend income and business profits. Multiple income streams help with building savings if the intelligent millennial investor has a robust savings strategy. So, while most millennial investors may not have rental income and higher dividend income streams yet, they may explore options such as starting a side hustle.

However, a concern on having a side hustle is that time invested in building additional streams might be better used to do better at your main job. Side hustles can be very distracting so there is a need for millennials to strike a balance between pursuit of money and have wonderful life experiences.

Most people are victims of lifestyle inflation. As their income increases, so do their lifestyle living expenses. The result is often more debt than they had before the income increase. A few years ago, I had a conversation with a co-worker who once worked for a top Canadian bank as an account manager. He was shocked to realize that, in general, most of the people who earned the six-figure incomes had more debt relative to their income compared to the middle-income earners. This points to the need for the intelligent millennial investor to be mindful of the impact of lifestyle inflation. Delayed gratification is key to building wealth over the long term. It seems easy in theory, but for most people it can be difficult to implement. Those with multiple income streams can increase their savings rate and their investment rate if they do not inflate their lifestyles.

Multiple income streams can be achieved by leveraging one's soft skills. This requires extra effort, and leveraging capital, labor, and technology. There is of course a tradeoff between leisure and time spent earning income. Generally, low-income people trade off their time for a fixed wage rate. The obvious limitation is that the wage is fixed for some time. As Eric Jorgenson noted in his 2020 book, *The Almanack of Naval Ravikant,* leveraging is a vehicle that can be used to increase income streams. Jorgenson further highlights that leveraging can be done through increasing capital, employing other people to scale up on work, and patenting one's innovations. Working an extra job increases one's capital. If one can optimally invest the employment income or capital borrowed from the bank, it can be turned into a source of multiple income streams.

Jeff Bezos, the founder of Amazon become a role model for success stories of my generation. His entrepreneurial prowess has attracted a huge following on social media. Entrepreneurs can leverage people through employing them to work for them and increasing the scale of production. While this may sound easy, being an entrepreneur is not a 9–5 job; it requires a lot of effort, which a few people like Jeff Bezos have been able to harness to become one of the richest people on earth. However, truth be told, entrepreneurship is not for everyone.

The advent of the internet has equalized the technology gap between rich and poor. A kid in the remote parts of Zimbabwe or India can now access the same information as a child in Canada, if they have access to the internet. A lot of millennials, especially social media influencers, have utilized streaming as a source of income. Influencers with huge followings are paid by advertisers, which can be another source of extra income. With the reach of the internet, most millennials have become aware of new ways of making extra money such as blogging or YouTubing.

To tap into the creator economy, I recently started my YouTube channel, Streetwise Economics, where I create content on personal finance and investing. I am learning every day that it is not an easy route. It requires some passion and dedication to achieve the monetization criteria.

Also, I have been following other leaders from Africa such as Fred Swaniker who has created ecosystems for young Africans through the African Leadership Academy (ALA) with interest in technology to learn technical skills such as coding. They can then potentially look for remote jobs in other countries such as Canada and the US, which offer relatively higher salaries. If one can work remotely from a location with a lower cost of living, and yet still get paid salaries like those in the developed countries, they can potentially have more income to invest if they do not inflate their lifestyle. The internet means one can work remotely for an employer despite any geographic boundary.

However, it is worth stressing the need for the Intelligent Millennial Investor to strike a balance between the pursuit of money and leisure. There is a tradeoff, especially if one is engaged in physically demanding labor like construction work, for example. I am aware of many folks who work more than one job and yet still complain of sinking in debt. Most of these jobs are minimum wage, which makes it hard to save a considerable proportion of their money. These kinds of stresses point to the importance of caring for our mental well-being. Even high-paying jobs require a lot of mental resilience, and no one is immune. As widely reported in mainstream media, Naomi Osaka (the world's number one tennis player) and gymnast Simone Biles bailed out of the Olympics gymnastics in Tokyo, 2021[30] for reasons related to mental wellbeing.

Starting a new business can also be a good way to build savings or to lose a lot of money. However, this is not for everyone. A Harvard Business Review article reported that approximately seven or eight out of ten new businesses fail to meet their projected rate of return.[31] So, I would encourage people who want to venture into business to get entrepreneurial training and avoid losing their money.

Most startups fail in the first five years of life. Many people make the mistake of thinking that working for another person is necessarily a bad thing. But not everyone can be like Elon Musk or Jeff Bezos, who have built and continue to build phenomenal multiple businesses that have become the envy of many millennials of my generation. The truth is, starting a business requires a lot of time, emotional intelligence, patience, unparalleled grit for identifying opportunities hidden in challenges, and in some cases the serendipity of a great network.[32] Starting a business is more than a 9–5 job. So, I encourage millennial investors to get entrepreneurial training before venturing into business of their own, to get some theoretical and practical experience.

The entrepreneurship situation has not been helped by the recent pop culture that has seen a lot of social media platforms such as Instagram, Meta, and YouTube full of young people flashing their 'wealth.' However, one popular singer, Akon, admitted in an interview with Al Jazeera that much of it is an illusion—pointing out, for example, that most people in the music industry shoot videos for their songs in beautiful, expensive cars that are *rented* and then immediately returned after the shoot is completed.

---

[30]https://www.cbc.ca/sports/olympics/summer/gymnastics/simone-biles-opts-out-of-floor-exercise-at-olympics-1.6125922.
[31]https://hbswk.hbs.edu/item/6591.html.
[32]https://www.lulu.com/en/ca/shop/isaac-jonas/the-serendipity-of-a-great-network/paperback/product-24430051.html?page=1&pageSize=4.

Unfortunately, some millennials attempt to emulate what they see on TV and rack up debt to try and look rich, and to the detriment of their personal finances. Nothing bad about that; however, if one is not careful and just buys for the sake of following the crowd, they may end up in debt simply out of a desire to keep up with the Joneses (FOMO). Dave Ramsey has pointed out that there is no need to compete with broke people. He even recommends folks in debt not even consider setting foot inside a restaurant until they pay off their debts. In short, he recommends avoiding debt, period. He had past experiences when he was almost buried alive in debt. Fortunately, he survived and has since turned that painful past into a way to build a better future. Before I go to the next chapter, I will share a summary and key thing to consider as a millennial investor in Canada.

Summary of the tax system in Canada

The tax system in Canada is a complex framework that involves multiple levels of government and various types of taxes. Below, I outline the key aspects of the tax system in Canada.

a) Types of taxes

There are different levels of taxes in Canada which include those levied and provincial and federal levels. These taxes are levied for different goals with policy makers such as the provincial and federal government. As an example, in addition to income taxes, there are other taxes in Canada, such as consumption taxes (e.g., Goods and Services Tax - GST), sales taxes, property taxes, and business taxes.

b) Progressive tax system

The Canadian tax system is progressive, meaning that the more income a person earns, the higher the percentage of income tax they pay. The income tax rates increase in steps or "brackets" as your income rises. I find helpful information on the Canadian taxes system following the link https://www.canada.ca/en/services/taxes.html.

c) Self-assessment

When I lived in Zimbabwe, the tax system was quite different. Other than the payroll and other taxes that were collected at point of sale, I did not have to self-report taxes at the end of the fiscal year as an individual. However, in Canada it is a different story. The Canadian tax system relies on self-assessment, where taxpayers are responsible for reporting their total income and determining their total tax owing. The Canada Revenue Agency (CRA) enforces tax laws through audits and penalties for errors or deliberate evasion[33].

d) Federal and provincial/Territorial taxes

Like I indicated in the paragraphs above, both the federal government and provincial/territorial governments levy income taxes. The federal government collects income taxes on behalf of all provinces and territories, except for Alberta, which collects its own corporate income taxes. Provincial governments also have the authority to levy direct taxes, such as property taxes.

e) Tax collection

The Canada Revenue Agency (CRA) is responsible for administering the federal income tax system. It collects personal and corporate income taxes, as well as other taxes, on behalf of the federal government and most provinces and territories. Quebec and Alberta have their own tax collection systems for corporate income taxes.

f) Taxation powers

Taxation powers in Canada are shared between the federal government and provincial/territorial legislatures. The federal government has broader taxation powers,

---

[33] https://www.legalline.ca/legal-answers/overview-of-the-canadian-tax-system/.

while provincial governments have more restricted authority for direct taxation within their respective provinces.

g) Tax credits and benefits

The Canadian tax system offers various tax credits and benefits for individuals, such as the Canada Child Benefit, GST/HST credit, disability tax credit, and more. These credits and benefits help reduce the overall tax burden for eligible individuals[34]. It is important to note that the tax system in Canada is subject to change, and it is advisable to consult official government sources or seek professional advice for specific tax-related matters.

h) Dividend income in Canada

Dividend income is treated differently from other types of income. However, the key highlights to understand as a millennial investor about how dividend income is treated in Canada are as follows: Depending on the types of dividends - dividends can be classified as eligible or non-eligible dividends. Eligible dividends are paid out of a

corporation's income that has already been taxed at the general corporate tax rate. On the other hand, non-eligible dividends, also known as ordinary dividends, come from income taxed at a lower small-business tax rate[35].

Taxation of dividends is done according to the type of dividend (eligible or non-eligible), the province an individual lives in, and also their marginal tax rate. The tax rates for eligible and non-eligible dividends vary, but generally, eligible dividends receive more favorable tax treatment[36].

Dividend gross-up and tax credit take effect when a person receives dividends, and the amount is subject to a dividend gross-up. This means that the dividend amount is

---

[34] https://www.canada.ca/en/services/taxes.html.
[35] https://turbotax.intuit.ca/tips/how-are-dividends-taxed-in-canada-16252.
[36] https://turbotax.intuit.ca/tips/how-are-dividends-taxed-in-canada-16252.

increased by a specific percentage before being included in your taxable income. However, to offset this gross-up, a dividend tax credit is provided, which helps reduce the overall tax liability on dividend income[37].

Depending on a person's provide of residence, provinces levy their own taxes with regards to dividend taxation. It is important to consider the specific tax regulations of your province when calculating the tax on dividend income[38].

In terms of foreign dividends, they may have different tax implications. I mostly invest most of my money in the US, so this rule affects me. The tax treatment of foreign dividends depends on various factors, including tax treaties between Canada and the country of origin of the dividends[39]. In my case, the tax for my investments in the US is withheld at source, so I receive the dividends net of tax.

Lastly, in this chapter, it is helpful to understand the various accounts one can invest in to reduce the cost of taxes which can ultimately reduce the return on investments. It is worthwhile to explore the following accounts for residents in Canada and the US.

Tax-advantaged accounts in Canada.

Tax-advantaged accounts are investment or savings accounts that can be used as vehicles to gain certain tax benefits, such as tax exemption or tax deferral. These accounts are designed to encourage individuals to save for specific purposes, such as retirement, education, or buying houses by providing favorable tax treatment. In both Canada there are various types of tax-advantaged accounts available.

---

[37] https://www.mmtcpa.ca/tax-tips/taxation-of-dividend-income/.
[38] https://turbotax.intuit.ca/tips/how-are-dividends-taxed-in-canada-16252.
[39] https://www.morningstar.ca/ca/news/185800/how-taxes-on-dividends-differ-.aspx.

Tax-advantaged accounts in Canada.

In Canada, some of the commonly known tax-advantaged accounts include:

a) Registered retirement savings plan

 A registered retirement savings plan (RRSP) is a personal savings plan that allows individuals to save for retirement while deferring taxes on the contributions made. Contributions to an RRSP are tax-deductible, and the investment growth within the account is tax-deferred until withdrawal. RRSP is a great vehicle to invest money and save towards retirement.

The RRSP also can be a source for individuals to borrow money if they want to pay towards home buying. However, it should be used for long-term investments because withdrawals from an RRSP before the age of 71 years are subject to taxation that depends on one's marginal tax rate. When an individual turns 71 years, the RRSP ends, and it must be converted to a Registered Retirement Income Fund (RRIF) or Life Income Fund (LIF).

The Canada Revenue Agency (CRA) generally calculates the RRSP limit and for 2024, the annual limit is calculated as 18% of earned reported income on the tax returns for the previous year, up to a maximum of $31,560[40].

b) Tax-free savings account

The tax-free savings account (TFSA) is a flexible savings account that allows individuals to earn tax-free investment income. Contributions to a TFSA are not tax-deductible, but any investment growth and withdrawals are tax-free. TFSA contributions are subject to an annual contribution limit, and it is adjusted yearly by CRA to adjust for inflation.

---

[40]https://www.canada.ca/en/revenue-agency/services/tax/individuals/topics/rrsps-related-plans/contributing-a-rrsp-prpp/contributions-affect-your-rrsp-prpp-deduction-limit.html.

In 2024 the TFSA yearly limit is $7,000 and it is calculated cumulatively from the time a person turns 18 years. Thus, a Canadian taxpayer who has never contributed to a TFSA and has been eligible for one since it was initiated will have a cumulative contribution room of $95,000.

c) Registered education savings plan

The registered education savings plan (RESP) is a savings plan especially designed to help individuals save for a child's post-secondary education. The contributions to a RESP are not tax-deductible, but the investment growth is tax deferred. When the funds are withdrawn for educational purposes, the earnings are taxed in the hands of the student, typically resulting in lower taxes due to their lower income. So, we have started investing for our child with the goal to build a financial nest egg for him when he goes to college.

d) Registered disability savings plan

A registered disability savings plan (RDSP) is a savings plan intended to help an individual who is approved to receive the disability tax credit (DTC) to save for their long-term financial security. Contributions to an RDSP are not tax deductible and can be made until the end of the year in which the beneficiary turns 59. Contributions that are withdrawn are not included as income to the beneficiary when paid out of an RDSP.

However, the Canada disability savings grant (grant), the Canada disability savings bond (bond), investment income earned in the plan, and the proceeds from rollovers are included in the beneficiary's income for tax purposes when paid out of the RDSP[41].

These are just a few examples of tax-advantaged accounts available in Canada. The specific rules and regulations governing these accounts may vary, so it is important to consult with a financial advisor or tax professional for personalized advice.

---

[41]https://www.canada.ca/en/revenue-agency/services/tax/individuals/topics/registered-disability-savings-plan-rdsp.html.

So, Canadians and Americans can benefit from investing into these different tax-advantaged accounts to help individuals save for retirement, education, and other specific purposes. These accounts provide tax benefits such as tax exemption or tax deferral, encouraging individuals to save and invest for their future. It is important to understand the specific rules and regulations governing these accounts and seek professional advice to make informed decisions based on individual circumstances. In concluding this chapter, I wanted to share a bit about life insurance because it is another important investment vehicle some families consider in their portfolio.

Life insurance

In Canada, life insurance is a financial product that provides a one-time, tax-free payment to your beneficiaries upon your death. It helps your loved ones deal with the financial impact of your passing by providing them with a lump-sum payment, known as a death benefit. This payment can be used for various purposes, such as replacing your income, providing for your children or dependents, paying off debts, covering funeral expenses, making charitable donations, or leaving money to your estate or a trust[42].

As such, there are different types of life insurance policies available in Canada, including term life insurance and permanent life insurance. Term life insurance provides coverage for a specific period, typically ranging from 10 to 40 years. It is often chosen to meet short-term financial needs, such as paying off a mortgage or putting children through college.

On the other hand, permanent life insurance offers lifetime coverage and may also build up a cash value over time[43]. When you purchase a life insurance policy, you enter into a contract with an insurance company. In exchange for paying a premium, the insurance company promises to pay the designated beneficiaries the agreed-upon death benefit

---

[42]https://www.canada.ca/en/financial-consumer-agency/services/insurance/life.html.
[43] https://lifeinsurancecanada.com/term-life-insurance.

upon your passing. The amount of coverage and the premium you pay depend on various factors, including your age, health, lifestyle, and the type of policy you choose[44].

In conclusion, the intelligent millennial investor should note that life insurance proceeds are generally not taxable in Canada. The lump-sum payment received by your beneficiaries is typically not subject to income tax[45]. To determine the right life insurance coverage for your needs, it is advisable to consult with a licensed insurance advisor who can provide personalized guidance based on your specific circumstances. This information can be searched online and also consult your financial institutions which may have these products. Caution should be taken that this information is general and is subject to change, so for more detailed and specific information, it is recommended to consult with a licensed insurance professional or refer to official government resources.

____

[44] https://timetoinvest.ca/insurance/life-insurance.
[45] https://timetoinvest.ca/insurance/life-insurance.

Chapter 5: The basics of the stock market

"Compound interest is the eighth wonder of the world. He who understands it, earns it, he who does not, pays it." Albert Einstein.

When I was growing up in rural Zimbabwe, I would hear my parents and community members discussing where they would sell or buy livestock. In Shona, my native language, they call it *"mariketi."* Recently, looking back to this experience, I have come to the realization that they were loosely referring to the "stock" market—a place where buyers and sellers of livestock physically met to transact business. Every community member who intended to sell livestock had to go through the process of obtaining authority from the village regulators and the neighborhood police services, who would clear the livestock before they could be sold.

On the other hand, the buyer would just show up with money and through an intermediary, a person cleared by the law enforcement authorities in my district, oversee the transactional process. Hence, at least once per year, the buyers and sellers of livestock would meet at a physical location agreed upon by the law enforcement authorities and finish their deals by the close of day.

Over the years, as a curious student of the markets and personal finance, I have come to appreciate how villagers back in rural Zimbabwe conducted such business transactions off-grid. However, when I started learning about the stock market in developed countries such as Canada and the US, I came to the realization that the principles my fellow villagers used are the same as those used globally in the major stock markets.

However, at the major stock markets where billions of shares of publicly listed companies are traded, naturally the process is conducted efficiently through advanced technology. An equivalent stock exchange like what my fellow villagers in Zimbabwe used to trade is like the Chicago Mercantile Exchange (CME) which trades commodities.

The other major stock markets in the US include the New York Stock Exchange (NYSE), the technology heavy weighted NASDAQ. In Canada there is the Toronto Stock

Exchange (TSX) and in China, the popular one is the Shanghai Stock Exchange. In simple terms, a stock exchange is where shares of publicly listed companies are traded. A publicly listed company is a business that is listed at a stock exchange where members of the public can trade their shares. In other words, a place where buyers and sellers of company shares meet to do the business of trading shares.

To ensure legality between stakeholders involved in the transactions, the stock exchanges are regulated by regulatory bodies. The regulatory bodies ensure fair rules are followed and monitor the exchanges to ensure there is no manipulation of transactions. For example, in the United States, the Securities Exchange Commission (SEC), an independent agency, enforces laws and regulations to ensure fairness in the US-based stock markets. On an average day, billions worth of trades exchange hands between stakeholders such as investors who may include institutional or individual investors, commonly known as retail investors.

To provide basic context, the US stock market has major indices such as the Standard and Poor's and Dow Jones. An index in the context of finance and investing, refers to a benchmark or a measurement tool used to track the performance of a specific market, market segment, investment strategy, or asset class. It provides a way to assess the overall movement and performance of a group of pre-selected investments, such as stocks, bonds, or other financial instruments.

The Standard and Poor's and the Dow Jones in the US are one of the most popular indices as I indicated in chapter four. They represent about eighty per cent of the top capitalized publicly listed companies in the US; hence most investors use it as a benchmark for performance of the stock market.

The origin of the Standard and Poor's Index dates to 1923 when it only had 233 companies represented in the index. In 1957, more companies were added to the index to make them five hundred. Hence from that time, it has been commonly referred to as the S&P 500 even though the number of listed companies can be slightly over five hundred, because some companies have multiple classes of stocks, such as Alphabet (Google).

In many stock exchanges around the world, investors have access to buy and sell shares of various securities such as individual stocks, Exchange Traded Funds (ETFs) and other fixed-income securities. An ETF is a pool of funds that are pooled together, such as mutual funds, or from institutions and individual investors and managed by a fund manager under a registered organization.

Popular funds include Berkshire Hathaway that has the legendary Warren Buffet as the Chief Executive Officer. Investing in an ETF offers some advantages such as low fees and has been yielding a higher return over the past decades, beating even most professional investors. There is also diversification as the ETF will buy shares of different stocks in the listed stock exchange and administer them under one fund.

These different securities have different returns on an annual basis. The access to the internet has enabled the intelligent millennial investor to have access to many investment securities including treasury bills. It is easy now to buy even US treasury bills online[46]. So, the intelligent millennial investor can consider owning some shares of ETFs that track the SPX through buying an ETF such as SPY as part of their investment portfolio. SPY is the ticker symbol. A stock ticker symbol is a unique series of letters assigned to a security for trading purposes. It is used to identify publicly traded companies on stock exchanges. Ticker symbols are often abbreviations that represent a company's name or its products.

---

[46]https://www.treasurydirect.gov/marketable-securities/treasury-bills/. Accessed online on 1 January 2023.

For example, "AAPL" is the ticker symbol for Apple Inc., and "WMT" is the symbol for Walmart.

Some investors can consider investing in funds such as the Berkshire Hathaway (BRK) that has consistently beaten the SPX in annual returns since 1964 when BRK was formed. BRK has two classes of shares, namely BRK-A and BRK-B with the class A shares being the most expensive.

Two classes of shares are a tier system that is created for various reasons including enabling individual (retail) investors to be able to buy some shares. Typically, fund managers have a lot of money running into millions of dollars so they can afford even the most expensive shares such as the BRK-A which goes for over half a million a share. As an example, most retail investors like me would afford the class B shares, which are currently trading at US$368.18/share as of close of business on January 8, 2024. In figure 5.1 on the next page, I show a graph comparing the BRK and S&P 500 Index returns on an annual basis from 1964-2022.

Fig 5.1 A graph showing the historical performance of Berkshire Hathaway Fund versus S&P 500 (1964-2022)

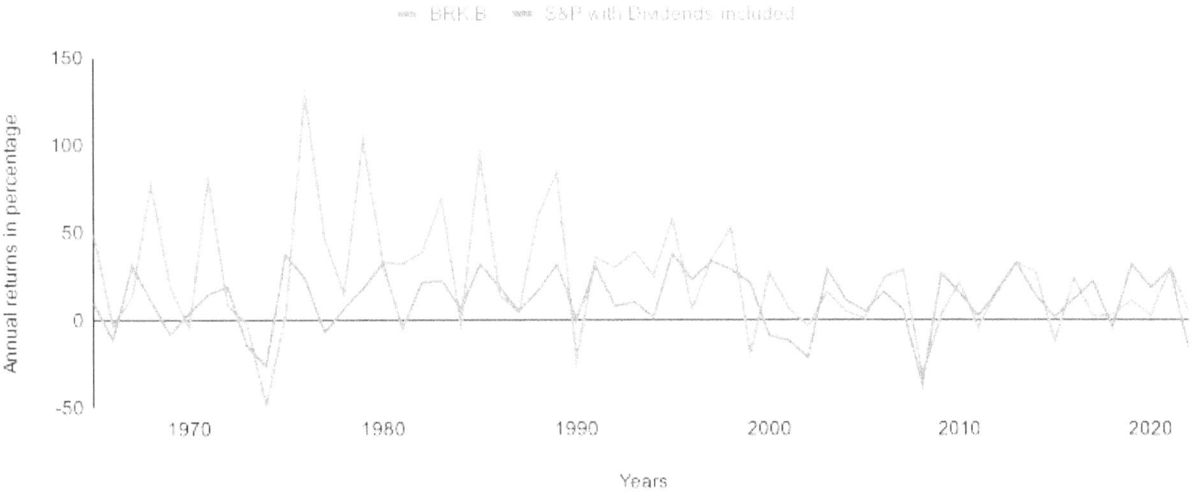

Source: Author's own graph with data from Berkshire Hathaway website.

Trading versus investing in the stock market.

Trading and investing are different, yet often confused. Before I get into the details, I will explain basic jargon that is used in the world of investing. Stock trading refers to the buying and selling of shares in publicly traded companies. When I buy shares of a company e.g Apple, I become a small part-owner of that company and have a claim on its assets and earnings. The value of the shares can fluctuate based on various factors, such as the company's financial performance, market conditions, and investor sentiment.

Stock trading takes place on stock exchanges, such as the New York Stock Exchange (NYSE) or the Nasdaq stock market. These exchanges provide a platform for buyers and sellers to trade shares. Traders closely monitor the short-term price changes of stocks and aim to buy low and sell high, seeking to profit from price movements. This short-term approach differentiates stock traders from long-term investors who hold onto their investments for an extended period.

To trade stocks, individuals can open brokerage accounts with licensed brokers or use online trading platforms. In my case, I use Questrade, and the platforms provide access to stock markets and allow me to place buy and sell orders for stocks. Some brokers even offer commission-free trading and the ability to buy fractional shares, making it more accessible for investors with smaller amounts of capital. For Questrade, they offer commission free for some ETFs and charge fees and or commissions for buying individual stocks and other securities.

It is important to note that stock trading involves risks, and it requires knowledge, research, and careful decision-making. It is advisable for new traders to seek guidance from experienced professionals or educate themselves on stock trading strategies and market dynamics. It is very possible to lose money if you do not understand how trading or investing works.

In summary, stock trading involves buying and selling shares of publicly traded companies on stock exchanges. Traders aim to profit from short-term price changes called technical analysis, while long-term investors focus on holding stocks for extended periods. It is important to understand the risks involved and consider seeking guidance when starting out.

Also, trading can be emotionally devastating, mainly because an amateur day trader will be competing with institutional investors who may use powerful computers and algorithms to trade. As well, watching the stock price fluctuating many times in one second can be extremely challenging for those who are faint-hearted. In most cases, once there is news about a certain stock or general guidance from policy makers such as the Fed or the central government, the intelligent millennial investor should be careful in following the crowd.

Speculation can also become an addictive habit regardless of the evidence in literature that points to lower rates of return on investments over the long term. However, there are some retail traders who may be good at it. Some may use swing trading, which involves buying and selling after one day. Swing trading is a speculative trading strategy whereby one holds a security for one or more days with the intention to profit from the price fluctuations.

Types of investments

The most common types of investment vehicles include equities such as stocks, mutual funds, ETFs and Index Funds, real estate, commodities such as wheat, oil etc., gold and silver, businesses, and cryptocurrencies. Cryptocurrencies have become popular with the news that inflation is forecast to increase. Investing in stocks represents ownership in a company. Owning shares entitles shareholder to certain rights, such as voting on company matters and receiving dividends if the company distributes them.

Investing in equities offers the potential for capital appreciation and income through dividends. When the value of the equities I own increases, I can sell them at a higher price and make a profit. Dividends, on the other hand, are a portion of the company's profits distributed to shareholders.

It is important to note that investing in equities carries risks. The value of equities can go up or down, and there is no guarantee of returns. As such, the millennial investors should carefully research and analyze companies before investing in their equities. Diversification and a long-term investment approach are often recommended to manage risk and potentially benefit from the growth of different companies and sectors.

As noted earlier, it is possible to trade or invest in bonds, mutual funds, real estate, commodities such as gold, and cryptocurrencies. The intelligent millennial investor can consider buying these investment asset classes when they are knowledgeable enough to understand how they can generate returns.

1. Individual stocks

Individual stocks are shares of publicly listed businesses. Examples of stock include Tesla, Amazon, and Netflix. When you own shares of individual businesses, or ETF, Index Funds or Mutual Funds, it means you own a piece of that business in which you are invested. Investing in individual stocks requires in-depth understanding of that business in terms of the product or service they offer, their competitive advantage, management, including the state of the business finances, and knowing when to buy to maximize the investor's profitability. I explain the key metrics to look at when considering investing in individual stocks under the psychology of investing in the next chapter.

2. Index funds

An index fund is a mutual fund or exchange-traded fund (ETF) designed to track a defined basket of investments. They come in various forms, such as actively or passively managed index funds. The most popular passively managed index fund in terms of share volumes is the Standard and Poor's Depositary Receipts (SPX) and the ETF that closely tracks it is identified by the ticker name SPY. Reminder: A ticker name is the unique letters that are assigned to a security for trading purposes on the stock exchange[47]. SPY essentially tracks the top 500 companies in the United States. Owning the SPY means that a shareholder will own a piece of shares of all the top 500 companies in the US over time. The Russell 2000 (IWM) is another common Index Fund that tracks the bottom 2000 companies of the US market. The Invesco QQQ Trust Series 1 (ticker name QQQ) is an index fund that tracks the top 100 non-financial companies on the NASDAQ stock exchange. Major holdings for the QQQ include Apple, Microsoft, Amazon, Tesla, and Facebook. Holding the QQQ index fund means owning a piece of all these businesses in the top 100 of the Nasdaq stock exchanges. The major advantage of *passively managed* index funds are their low management fees, which can increase the compounded rate of return over the long term.

On the other hand, the *actively managed* funds have higher management fees. Basically, the fund manager is paid for actively trading the securities holdings in the exchange-traded funds. The goal of actively trading the security holdings is to try and beat the benchmark, such as the S&P 500. Historically, only in rare cases have fund managers been able to beat the benchmark index such as the S&P 500 index; just 15 percent of fund managers have managed to consistently beat the S&P benchmark for the decade ending in 2019[48].

The most popular actively managed ETF since the COVID-19 pandemic has been the Ark funds managed by Cathie Wood. However, the fund has plummeted since February 2021 owing to sector rotation of money from stocks of companies that benefited from staying at home as opposed to the traditional defensive stocks such as banks. The successful vaccination rollout in developed economies such as Canada and the US has resulted in most investors shifting into other undervalued sectors such as energy, banks, and travel and entertainment.

---

[47]https://shorturl.at/eJMOT. Accessed online on 23 January 2024.
[48]https://www.cnbc.com/2019/03/15/active-fund-managers-trail-the-sp-500-for-the-ninth-year-in-a-row-in-triumph-for-indexing.html.

3. Mutual funds

A mutual fund is an investment vehicle that allows individuals to pool their money with other investors to collectively invest in a diversified portfolio of stocks, bonds, or other securities. These funds are managed by professional money managers who make investment decisions on behalf of the investors. Here are some key points to consider about mutual funds.

a) Investment structure

When I invest in a mutual fund, I will be essentially buying shares of the fund. The value of these shares, known as the net asset value (NAV), is determined by dividing the total value of the fund's assets by the number of shares outstanding.

b) Diversification

Mutual funds are usually diversified in terms of the asset classes they own. This is one of the main advantages of mutual funds is their ability to provide diversification. By pooling money from multiple investors, mutual funds can invest in a wide range of securities, spreading the risk across different asset classes, sectors, and geographies.

c) Professional management

Mutual funds are managed by professional money managers who have expertise in analyzing and selecting investments, for a fee or commission which can be at least 2 per cent per year. Fees and Expenses for mutual funds cover expenses to administer and manage the fund. These fees can include management fees, administrative fees, and distribution fees. It is important to carefully review the fund's prospectus to understand the fees associated with investing in a particular mutual fund. These fees can often reduce the overall return for investors if they are quite high. In my case, I manage my own investments and reduce the professional fees. As a word of caution, it is important to understand how to invest otherwise one can lose all their money. These managers make decisions on which securities to buy, hold, or sell based on the fund's investment objectives and strategies.

Types of mutual funds

There are various types of mutual funds available, each with its own investment focus and strategy. Some common types include equity funds (investing in stocks), bond funds (investing in bonds), balanced funds (investing in a mix of stocks and bonds), index funds (tracking a specific market index), and sector funds (investing in specific sectors of the economy).

Income and capital gains

Mutual funds and investment in other equities and or securities generate income through interest, dividends, and capital gains from the securities held in their portfolios. This income is distributed to the fund's shareholders in the form of dividends or reinvested back into the fund.

Accessibility

Mutual funds are widely accessible to individual investors, and one can typically invest in them through financial institutions, such as banks, brokerage firms, or directly from the fund company. The minimum investment amount and availability of different funds may vary.

4. Gold and silver

Investors invest in gold and silver mainly through the index funds that track these commodities. The major advantage of gold is that it cannot be printed like money, which can be produced by central banks through Quantitative Easing (QE). By buying and owning gold, storage, and insurance costs of keeping it safely can be an extra burden. If I physically own gold, I will need to store it safely and insure it against loss or damage. These costs can add to the overall cost of your investment and should be considered when evaluating the potential returns of holding gold. Nonetheless, some investors still consider commodities such as gold and silver an effective hedge against inflation. I stay out of commodity markets (except gold ETF) as I do not understand them as well as I would need to for comfort. The gold ETF in my portfolio acts as a hedge against inflation.

Gold and equities historically move in opposite directions. The relationship between gold and equities, or stocks, can vary and is not always predictable. However, there are some instances where gold and equities may move in opposite directions. Here are a few possible reasons:

a) Safe-haven asset vs. risk-on asset

Gold is often considered a safe-haven asset, meaning that investors tend to flock to it during times of economic uncertainty or market volatility. On the other hand, equities are generally considered risk-on assets, as their value is tied to the performance of companies and the overall economy. During periods of market stress or economic downturns, investors may sell equities and move their investments into gold as a way to preserve capital, leading to a negative correlation between the two.

b) Inverse relationship with the U.S. dollar

Gold is priced in U.S. dollars, and there is often an inverse relationship between the value of the U.S. dollar and the price of gold. When the U.S. dollar depreciates, the price of gold tends to rise, and vice versa. Equities, on the other hand, can be influenced by a variety of factors, including company performance, economic indicators, and investor sentiment. This can lead to situations where gold and equities move in opposite directions. If this happens, it can potentially act as an advantage to an investor unlike a situation when the whole portfolio drops. It can lead to a major drawdown in the portfolio.

c) Market sentiment and investor behavior

Market sentiment and investor behavior can also play a role in the relationship between gold and equities. During periods of optimism and bullish market sentiment, investors may be more inclined to invest in equities, driving their prices higher. Conversely, during periods of pessimism or fear, investors may seek the perceived safety of gold, leading to a divergence in the performance of gold and equities.

5. Cryptocurrencies

Cryptocurrency is a form of digital or virtual currency that uses cryptography to secure transactions and control the creation of new units. It operates on decentralized networks, typically using blockchain technology, which is a distributed ledger maintained by a network of computers. I explain a few important concepts that are associated with cryptocurrencies.

a) Decentralization

Cryptocurrencies are not issued or regulated by any central authority, such as a government or central bank. Instead, they rely on decentralized systems, where transactions are verified and recorded by a network of computers, making them theoretically immune to government interference or manipulation.

b) Security and privacy

Cryptocurrencies use cryptographic techniques to secure transactions and control the creation of new units. This makes them highly secure and resistant to counterfeiting or fraud. Additionally, cryptocurrencies can offer a certain level of privacy, as transactions can be pseudonymous, meaning they are not directly linked to the identities of the individuals involved.

c) Digital payments

Cryptocurrencies enable peer-to-peer transactions, allowing anyone, anywhere to send and receive payments without relying on traditional financial intermediaries like banks. These transactions are recorded in a public ledger, known as the blockchain, which provides transparency and immutability.

d) Investment and speculation

Cryptocurrencies have gained popularity as investment assets. Some people buy and hold cryptocurrencies with the expectation that their value will increase over time. However, it is important to note that the value of cryptocurrencies can be highly volatile, and investing in them carries risks.

e) Wide range of cryptocurrencies

Bitcoin, launched in 2008, was the first and remains the most well-known cryptocurrency. However, there are now thousands of different cryptocurrencies, each with its own features and use cases. Some popular cryptocurrencies include ethereum, litecoin, ripple, and bitcoin cash. Today as I am writing this book on February 12, 2024, the price of one bitcoin price is above CAD 69,000 and of course it can fluctuate overtime.

f) Use cases.

Cryptocurrencies can be used for various purposes beyond traditional payments. They have the potential to streamline financial transactions, enable faster cross-border transfers, facilitate smart contracts, and provide solutions to existing financial system shortcomings. The underlying blockchain technology also has applications in industries beyond finance, such as supply chain management and decentralized internet.

As a word of caution, it is important to note that while cryptocurrencies offer potential benefits, they very well come with risks and rewards. The risks include regulatory uncertainties, market volatility, security vulnerabilities, and the potential for fraudulent activities. The potential reward could be the upside resulting in some realized profits by the investor. Therefore, it is advisable to thoroughly research and understand the specific cryptocurrency you are interested in and consider consulting with a financial advisor before making any investment decisions.

6. Real estate

The intelligent millennial investor can invest in real estate, as explained in Chapter 2. Another way to invest in real estate is through Real Estate Investment Trusts (REITs). These are index funds for securities in real estate. The advantage of investing in REITs is there is no huge down payment required to buy the securities, as opposed to buying real estate. Also, REITs can pay dividends immediately, which is an advantage. In Canada and the United States there are a lot of REITs, which may be good investment vehicles. The key is to be aware of the major holdings and risk exposure for the REITs and to know your risk tolerance.

Risk tolerance in investing

Risk tolerance refers to the level of risk an investor is willing to endure in their investment portfolio given any level of volatility. There are moments when portfolio value can fluctuate as the holdings therein fluctuate in value. So, this is an important part of investing because some investors may struggle to handle the major drops in the stock market while others can do so comfortably. So, in short, risk tolerance reflects an individual's ability to handle potential losses and uncertainty associated with investing. It is an important factor in determining the type and amount of investments an individual chooses. Understanding one's risk tolerance is important to building a portfolio that aligns with one's comfort level and investment goals. Every person has a different risk tolerance. I like to have a yearlong worth of emergence fund so that I can right off any short-term drawdown in the long-term portfolio. I explain important concepts as they relate to risk tolerance below.

Factors affecting risk tolerance

There are several factors that influence an investor's risk tolerance. These include the investor's time horizon, investment goals, income level, investment knowledge and experience, financial situation, and personal attitudes towards risk.

a) Time horizon

The length of time an investor has to achieve their investment goals can impact their risk tolerance. Generally, investors with longer time horizons, such as those saving for retirement, may have a higher risk tolerance as they have more time to recover from potential losses. I am approaching 4o years now plus I have a young child, so my risk tolerance is now declining. I am now much more conservative than I was in my earlier 20s and before I had a family of my own. Now, I have to be more careful with securities. I invest the family income to avoid ruinous risk which can put the whole family in financial jeopardy.

b) Investment goals

The specific goals an investor has, such as capital preservation, income generation, or long-term growth, can influence their risk tolerance. Different investment goals may require different levels of risk exposure. At this point of my life, my goal is to preserve the capital and grow it so that my family's retirement portfolio grows for us to retire early and focus on other projects we are passionate about.

c) Investment knowledge and experience

An investor's level of knowledge and experience in investing can affect their risk tolerance. Those with more knowledge and experience may be more comfortable taking on higher levels of risk. When I started investing on my own in the stock market in 2020, I have learnt quite a bit and there is still a lot more for me to learn. The key thing I have learnt is to manage risk and stay humble because conditions in the stock market can evolve very fast.

d) Emotional and behavioral factors

Risk tolerance is also influenced by an individual's emotional and behavioral tendencies. Some investors may be more risk-averse and prefer lower-risk investments, while others may be more comfortable with higher levels of risk and potential returns.

Hence, determining your risk tolerance involves assessing your comfort level with potential losses, considering your investment goals, and understanding your financial situation. Various financial institutions and online resources offer risk tolerance questionnaires that can help you assess your risk tolerance level.

I have also learnt that it is important to take away emotions from investing in the stock market. The market has no emotions. It is also important to note that risk tolerance is a personal and subjective measure, and it can change over time as your circumstances and investment goals evolve. Regularly reviewing and reassessing your risk tolerance is essential to ensure your investment strategy remains aligned with your comfort level and objectives. Next, I explain how to have a rule to compound an investor's portfolio.

The Power of compound interest (Rule of 72)

The rule of 72 is a simple and useful tool for estimating the time it will take for an investment to double in value based on a fixed annual rate of return. The formula for the Rule of 72 is:

$$Years = 72/Rate\ of\ Return\ on\ Investment\ (or\ interest\ rate)$$

It is important to note that the rule of 72 is an approximation and may not be perfectly accurate, especially as the interest rate deviates from 8 percent. The farther the interest rate is from 8 percent, the less precise the results will be. For continuous compounding, using 69.3 in the numerator can provide a more accurate result. Some people adjust this to 69 or 70 for the sake of easy calculations.

It is worth noting that the rule of 72 is a convenient approximation for estimating the doubling time for an investment, and it can provide a quick and easy way to assess the potential growth of an investment based on a fixed rate of return.

The most common misconception out there is that a person needs a lot of upfront money to build wealth. While a few fortunate individuals may have been born into wealthy families, an intelligent millennial investor can build wealth from scratch overtime. Amongst many other ways to build wealth, an intelligent millennial investor can leverage the power of compound interest, be psychologically disciplined in managing their portfolio, optimize taxes by investing in right accounts, and improve skills to increase earning power. As I am writing this book, I am taking an online course on how to trade options. I had to pay fees and also learn from instructors who do it for a living and are experienced.

Options are financial contracts that give investors the right, but not the obligation, to buy or sell an underlying asset at a predetermined price within a given time period. They are considered derivatives because their value is derived from the underlying asset, such as stocks, commodities, currencies, or bonds[49].

Types of options

There are two main types of options: (i) call options and, (ii) put options.

Call options give the holder the right to buy the underlying asset at a specified price, known as the strike price, before the expiration date. On the other hand, call options are typically used when investors believe the price of the underlying asset will rise. In doing so, put options give the holder the right to sell the underlying asset at the strike price before the expiration date. Put options are commonly used when investors anticipate that the price of the underlying asset will decrease.

How options work

Options provide investors with flexibility and the ability to implement various trading strategies. Because options are leveraged on the underlying stocks, they are riskier than trading stocks. However, if there is a price movement in the direction the investor is betting for, it can result in much higher profit compared to the same investment in the underlying stock. In trading options, it is important to understand the following terms:

1. Expiration Date: Options have a specific expiration date, after which they become worthless. Investors must exercise their options before the expiration date if they want to buy or sell the underlying asset at the strike price.

---

[49] https://www.schwab.com/options/what-is-trading-options,

2. Strike Price: The strike price is the predetermined price at which the underlying asset can be bought or sold. It is agreed upon when the option contract is created.

3. Premium: When buying options, investors pay a premium, which is the cost of the option contract. The premium is influenced by factors such as the current price of the underlying asset, the time remaining until expiration, and market volatility.

4. Leverage: Options allow investors to control a larger amount of the underlying asset with a smaller investment. This leverage can amplify potential gains but also increase the risk of losses.

5. Risk Management: Options can be used for risk management purposes, such as hedging existing investments. For example, an investor who owns stock can buy put options to protect against a potential decline in the stock's price.

6. Complexity: Options can be complex and difficult to understand for inexperienced investors. It is important to fully understand the potential risks and implications before trading options.

Compound interest is the interest earned on the initial principal amount, as well as the interest that accumulates over time. It is a compounding effect that allows investments to grow faster. Imagine planting a tree, and then the tree matures and produces seeds. The seeds may then be planted again and grow, repeating the sequence until a forest is created. Compound interest works in a similar way. The major temptation for an intelligent millennial investor to avoid is speculation, as it can be potentially catastrophic in terms of return on investment in the long term. Speculation has proven to lead to lower returns in the long term due to the higher trading fees and the impacts of many unknowns that are associated with speculating. Hence one of the challenges for intelligent millennial investors is to perform due diligence before investing or speculating in securities.

Taking advantage of compound interest is a powerful tool that can be used to build wealth. However, it is worth mentioning that compound interest works in two ways. First, if the intelligent millennial investor is receiving the interest, they can build wealth. Conversely, if they are paying interest, it can make them poorer. Hence, to be on the side of building wealth, the intelligent millennial investor can develop an investment strategy that ensures they are on the receiving end of interest from investments, rather than the reverse.

To take advantage of compound interest, one can focus on factors such as the principal and consistency of investing money in the stock market. Compound interest can be calculated using the following equation:

$$A \ = \ P(1 \ + \ \frac{r}{n})^{nt}$$

A is the final amount to be realized in a defined period say 10 years. *P* is the initial principal balance which can be an initial deposit of money in the stock market or bank. The *r* is the rate of interest per period e.g., per month or a year. We can set n=1 for a start and t is the number of periods. So, the *Rule of 72* is a simple way to estimate the time an investment will take to double given a fixed rate of interest.

An intelligent millennial investor can apply a simple approach to building wealth by focusing on the things they can control, such as increasing their earning potential by building their skills sets, taking an extra job to have multiple streams of income, and taking advantage of investing early on, while still young and controlling their spending.

An intelligent millennial investor may choose to take a passive investing approach and invest most of their money in the ETFs that track the SPX, buy a few shares of fundamentally strong companies at a discount, and consistently do it over time, and invest in real estate by buying a house. It is also important to first tax shelter the investment by putting money in registered accounts such as the TFSA for Canadians or the Roth IRAs for US residents, before investing in the unregistered accounts. I must also state that investing in stocks and other investments carries some risk. This risk can include but is not limited to the following;

1. Market risk

Successful investing in the stock market requires investors to carefully consider their investment objectives and risk tolerance before investing. Owning stocks and investment securities such as index funds and individual stocks comes with inherent market risks as these securities fluctuate in value over time in response to many factors such as missing expected earnings or external factors such as changing interest rates or investor sentiments. So, one should prepare for ups and downs throughout the time they will be invested in the stock market.

2. Inflation risk

Investing in stocks may be affected by inflation as the value of the assets may be eroded by rising prices over time. Generally, inflation levels in Canada and the US have been low, with their central banks targeting an annual inflation rate of 2 per cent. However, in a period of high inflation like what happened in 2023, inflation can go up to as much as 8 percent a year. In 1920, inflation level reached an all-time high of 21.60 percent[50].

3. Credit risk

Investing in stocks and bonds exposes investors to credit risk. As an example, Index funds or mutual funds holding more than one stock in their portfolio may experience credit risk if one of their holdings goes bankrupt. It is even riskier if an investor is invested in only one stock, which files for bankruptcy. That is why it is a good idea to diversify in businesses one understands, to spread the risk in case of business failure.

4. Liquidity risk

Investment securities such as stocks and bonds may pose liquidity risk if they have low average trading volumes per day. There are some stocks and ETFs such as Tesla and SPY that are highly liquid, averaging millions of shares traded in a day. On the opposite end of the spectrum, there are some securities that may not have many trades per day in terms of their share volumes. Such that, it may pose risk if the investor may want to buy or sell shares, due to market conditions or other factors.

---

[50] https://tradingeconomics.com..

Chapter 6: How to pick stocks for investing

My first experience with the subject of psychology was in 2008 at the University of Zimbabwe. I undertook an Introduction to Psychology course as an elective for my undergraduate degree in economics. Thirteen years later, vivid memories of my first day in class include the lecturer for this course, Mr. Mudzwiti. The first day, he arrived at the podium and started off by setting out his ground rules. Two of the rules included zero tolerance for cell phone ringing and disapproval of latecomers to the lecture. He emphasized that any transgression of those two rules would be consequential to the whole class. He did not say what the penalty would be.

As I now look back, I see that the lecturer was training the students to follow certain rules and behave in a certain way. Also, every behavior had a risk or reward. Similarly, in the world of investing, as economist Benjamin Graham wrote, Mr. Market is bipolar. He is sometimes moody and sometimes happy. It is simply hard to read his next mood. This is key because a lot of investors lose money by thinking they can predict the direction of the market in the short term, and consequently take too much risk.

Similarly, investing in the capital markets requires participants to make some assumptions which can act as rules or guidelines in their investment journey. Some of the assumptions that I follow when investing in the stock markets are based on the fact that, capital markets are where savings and investments are channeled between suppliers and those in need. Suppliers typically include banks and investors, while those seeking capital can be businesses, governments, and individuals. This interaction between the various stakeholders creates a market that can potentially generate billions of profits of participants.

The most common capital markets are the stock market and the bond market, where different financial instruments, including equities and debt, are traded. When I invest, I mostly do so in the stock market where I buy stocks and bonds for long term investments. Once in a while if I see good opportunities, I can trade stocks in the short term. So, when I invest, I use the following guidelines:

1) My base currency is the Canadian dollar. However, I mostly invest in the US stock market so I will have my broker exchange the Canadian dollars to United States dollars so that I will be able to buy US dollar denominated assets.

2) I have different investment objectives, risk target, investment opportunity set, and investment horizon when sizing allocations to the capital markets. For much of my portfolio, I invest with a long term in mind and my risk tolerance is conservative. That is, I balance my portfolio between equities and bonds and cash. Cash is available to be allocated when there are buying opportunities for equities or bonds.

So, as millennial investors, it is important to have clear investment goals and understand risk tolerance. This is so because every move one makes in the market has a risk or reward return. The late Kenny Rogers song, *The Gambler*, contains an applicable catchy phrase: *"You've got to know when to hold them. Know when to fold 'em. Know when to walk away. Know when to run."*[51]

Similarly, I have learned that with investing, it is helpful to be aware of one's behavior and the bigger picture. It is also equally instructive to know when to hold up, when to run, and when it is time to walk away. One of the key things that influences an investor's success is behavior, especially in the face of fast-changing market conditions.

When stock markets around the world dropped starting in October 2022 when central banks in Canada and US started increasing the interest rates, to contain fast rising inflation, there was panic and as the stock market dropped, there was a massive sell-off

---

[51]https://www.youtube.com/watch?v=7hx4gdlfamo&ab_channel=KennyRogersVEVO.

of stocks mostly in the technology sector in the US and Canadian markets, up until the second quarter of 2023. I remember looking at my portfolio being 30 per cent down and I actually kept on buying stocks with good fundamentals and major indexes like SPY and Berkshire Hathaway. By the end of the year, as with most investors who had held up, my portfolio was up over 45% for 2023 compared to where it was at the beginning of the year. The story here is that there were a lot of people who panicked, and this is usually exacerbated by the headlines and pundits who seem to suggest that they can predict the future. The logical thing for the Millennial investor to do during this time would have been to buy, contrary to the behavior of the crowd, after having done their homework, as I will explain below.

COVID-19 started in Wuhan, China around December 2019 when the first public reports of the virus surfaced in the international news headlines; the United States (US) stock market began to drop on February 2020[52] and within four trading days, it had recorded a 26 percent drop, with the Dow Jones (DJ) plunging 6,400 points in a single day. This drop in the major stock markets of the world sent shockwaves of fear to most investors. Most investors, as indicated by the investor sentiment and the extent of sell-off in the stock market, seemed to believe that people would be wiped out.

On the other hand, a few smart investors saw the stock market correction as one of the best moments to get into the market at the unusually low point and make money. The intelligent millennial investor should also remember that, for all investors, the key is to *buy low and sell high*. As Warren Buffet, one of the best investors of all time, said, "When everyone gets greedy be fearful, and be greedy when everyone gets fearful." Those who understand the game well prefer to buy when there is "blood in the streets," that is, when the market is red, and sell when it is green.

---

[52]https://www.sciencedirect.com/science/article/pii/S1544612320306668.

Investing in the stock market can be a complicated process, especially given the associated risk. Consequently, that is when a strong understanding of investing principles and the psychology behind investing can be effective for the intelligent millennial investor. Too often people lose money due to behavioral factors such as impatience, fear, and greed. As noted earlier, the stock market is unpredictable, at least in the short term.

However, historically, the stock market has been a consistent vehicle to create wealth in the advanced economies such as Canada and US, for those who are patient. Investing in the stock markets seems simple when one looks back in hindsight. Hence, even in the heat of the moment and without the benefit of hindsight, an intelligent millennial investor can still take advantage of corrections in the market. Depending on one's investment strategy, some people are more comfortable letting financial managers manage their money, as these managers may be perceived as having more hands-on experience. On the other hand, for those who may choose to take the Do-It-Yourself (DIY) approach, which is self-directed investing, it is important to understand how the global economy works. Just like everything in life, each approach has merits and demerits.

If choosing the DIY approach, it is important for the intelligent millennial investor to spend some time acquiring education on how the markets function in general. This is not an easy task but with the advent of the internet there are a lot of useful resources to be found. The internet has become the equalizer, at least for those who can access it. One can learn trading or investing online from any part of the world if there is internet access.

However, due care should be taken when choosing relevant information because of the volume of online material, some of which is misleading or erroneous. In my case, I am careful of scammers and people who reach out to me wanting to have them invest my money and promise very high investment returns. The SPX which has returned one of the highest investment returns around the world, on average returns about 9% per year. So, when I see a person who comes to me offering returns that are higher than the SPX,

I become extra careful with my money. So, I find the Canadian banks to be safer to invest with if one is not comfortable with self-directed investing.

In terms of searching for the helpful content on investing in the stock market, a simple search on YouTube under the heading of "investing" can generate many thousands of videos. So, I particularly research about the profile of those people who make the videos and have an idea if they may have had a successful career or record of accomplishment as investors. I have come to access the YouTube videos by former financial advisors or experienced investors such as Ray Dalio - founder of Bridgewater Associates hedge fund. I have also watched several videos from Warren Buffet and the late Charlie Munger.

There are also numerous good books written by most of the successful investors, such as Ray Dalio and Warren Buffet, who have written numerous letters to shareholders which are on Berkshire Hathaway's website. I have found the annual shareholder letters very helpful in understanding how Berkshire Hathaway picks stocks and their investment thesis such as some portion of their portfolio in cash having, sometimes at least 20% to take advantage of the unexpected fluctuations in the stock market. Too often, particularly good businesses will be selling at huge discounts when there is too much fear in the market as gauged by the Greed and Fear Index.

The Fear and Greed Index is a tool used to gauge the mood of the market and assess investor sentiment. It is designed to help investors understand the emotional and reactionary aspects of market behavior, particularly the influence of fear and greed on investment decisions.

Choosing a winning investment strategy

There are over 1,600 companies listed on the Toronto Stock Exchange and over 3,767[53] domestically listed companies in the Nasdaq stock exchange alone in the US. So, how does one choose where to invest out of all such options? The first thing is to have a

---

[53] https://focus.world-exchanges.org/articles/number-listed-companies#:~:text=At%20the%20end%20of%20Q1,EMEA%20for%20the%20rest%2025%25.

defined investing strategy and then use technology to filter through all these many companies, searching for securities that meet the minimum requirements of one's investment strategy.

Investing in the stock market requires a strategy; preferably a long-term view of building wealth that can then be broken down into small actionable steps in the present. My number 1 rule is I *do not gamble with my money*. In other words, I do not invest in securities I do not understand. Rule number 2 is read number 1, again. Why gamble with your hard-earned money? It is also key for the intelligent millennial investor to appreciate individual risk tolerance levels.

However, for those who choose the DIY approach, one simply needs access to a stable internet connection, a brokerage account, a laptop, or a mobile phone that can access the internet, and some knowledge of which securities to buy. The most common brokerage account in Canada is Questrade, and banks also offer investing services. Banks also offer DIY services for those who want to have more control in managing their finances. However, my research shows that most banks charge higher transaction fees compared to Questrade.

If one is knowledgeable, the advantage of DIY is that it offers an opportunity to pay lower fees compared to institutional investing, as well as the advantage of taking control of one's financial destiny rather than leaving it to someone else. In the United States, there are plenty of brokerage firms such as Interactive Brokers, Charles Schwab Fidelity Investments, and Robinhood, at one point one of the most popular with millennials.

Robinhood is popular for its 'no-fee' approach and for enabling retail investors to buy fractional shares for stocks they otherwise could not afford to buy.

A simple rule of thumb I use when investing in the stock market is to perform your own due diligence before investing in any security. I as much as possible stay in your circle of competence and read widely. As a simple starting point, ask yourself: In my household, what gadgets do we have? A phone, a computer or internet. That might point to the Apple iPhone, Apple computer, and Google for internet. These three are all listed companies in the stock exchange, with publicly tradable shares. Helpful journals for investment reading may include *The Wall Street Journal, The New York Times, Barrons, The Financial Times*, and *The Globe and Mail*, especially for Canadian investors.

In his classic book, *The Intelligent Investor,* Benjamin Graham outlines the salient principles that an intelligent millennial investor can apply to maximize return on investment. These principles are Meaning, Moat, Management and Margin of Safety, hereafter referred to as the Four M's.

1. Meaning

When the intelligent millennial investor invests in securities, owning a piece of that business. Hence if they have values they want to support, they can vote with their money through buying shares of businesses whose values align with theirs. One example is that of Tesla. Many millennial investors invest in the company as they believe the company is solving a generational problem of climate change by powering vehicles with clean energy. This may explain why millennials continue to buy Tesla stock even though most analysts agree that the company is overvalued. This is one principle that I apply in addition to others I have described such as margin of safety, management etc. As an example, I do not invest in companies that produce cigarettes or tobacco products.

The issue of valuation is a difficult one, and the intelligent millennial investor is encouraged to educate themselves on the most popular valuation models such as the Discount Cash Flow model (DCM) and Earnings Per Share (EPS). The DCM is simply an attempt to measure the value of the business by estimating the future cash flows and fundamentals of how much money the business will make in the future. Again, it is important to understand that this is an estimate with a range of possible share values.

The formula to calculate the DCM is as follows:

$$DCM = \frac{CF1}{(1+r)^{\wedge}1} + \frac{CF2}{(1+r)^{\wedge}2} + \cdots + \frac{CFn}{(1+r)^{\wedge}n}$$

Where r is the estimated discount rate and CF1, CF2 and CFn are estimated cash flows for year 1, 2 and additional years, respectively. A discount rate is used to determine the present value of future cash flows per share. It represents the rate of return required by an investor to justify the investment. Hence by discounting future cash flows back to their present value, the DCF analysis helps assess the attractiveness and financial viability of an investment.

The earnings per share (EPS) method is a financial metric used to assess a company's profitability and measure its earnings on a per-share basis. It provides insight into the portion of a company's profit that is allocated to each outstanding share of common stock. The EPS method essentially is premised on the theory that investors will invest in the business if they believe their earnings will grow in the future and vice versa. So, it is also key to compare with the EPS for peers in the sector of the business the investor will be investing in.

$$EPS = \frac{Net\ Income - Preferred\ Dividends}{Weighted\ Average\ Number\ of\ Shares\ Outstanding}$$

All the information in the formula is obtainable in the financial statements which are publicly available. For example, searching online for Tesla financial statements can be found on their website on the link[54]. The key is to understand how to interpret the numbers. All listed companies in Canada and the US are required by law to file audited financial statements by their respective regulators.

---

[54]https://ir.tesla.com/press-release/tesla-releases-third-quarter-2023-financial-results.

2. Moat

An intelligent millennial investor can also investigate a company's moat. A moat is simply a competitive advantage a company may have relative to the market. This competitive advantage may be the result of a huge scale such as Alphabet Inc., which is a pioneer in the internet search space thanks to two Stanford graduate students, Larry Page, and Sergey Brin, who started this company in 1998. As the leader in the internet provision space, Alphabet Inc. may be able to set their price and drive their competitors out of the market. In the e-commerce space, Amazon has a moat.

Amazon as an example has been growing into different segments and competing with physical retailers such as Walmart. With the COVID-19 pandemic, most customers preferred shopping online due to lockdowns and due to the benefits of time savings that accrue from online shopping. So, it has a competitive advantage in the online retail sector, and it is also growing in other segments such as cloud computing and data storage.

So, an intelligent millennial investor may be able to purchase a stock with a moat like Amazon at a discount price when there is a drop in sticker price and enjoy the benefits of compounding return over the long term. I was able to buy some shares for Amazon at the beginning of 2023, at a discount because the shares were over 30% down at some point from their previous 52 week high. You can see on the graph below that, around the beginning of 2023, it dropped to about $85.25/share which was a huge discount in my view based on their earnings and cash flows Amazon has generated over the past years.

The cash flows can be found in the Cash Flow statement, and I look at the free cash flows because if a business can generate cash flows, then, I believe they will be able to meet their financial needs such as debt repayment and even operational needs.

Fig 6.0. The graph shows the stock price fluctuations for Amazon over the past 5 years.

Source: Google Finance as of 9 January 2024

Stock ticker price is the price of a security that is shown when it is being traded. The key thing is to estimate the intrinsic value (true value) of the stock. Intrinsic value of a stock is the true value of a security when all fundamentals are considered.

Investing in a stock with a moat at a good price offers several advantages. One advantage is the potential for a higher return and less risk of bankruptcy and subsequent loss of money. Conversely, investing in a company that does not have a competitive advantage can have disadvantages as it may lose market share.

3. Management

The devil is in the details; hence, the intelligent millennial investor should investigate the management of the companies they want to invest in. With new tools such as the Rule one toolbox[55], it is possible to get all the latest insider transitions and top leadership trading details. The advantage of investing in publicly listed companies is that these companies are obligated to follow regulations set out by the regulatory authorities. For example, in the United States market, the Security Exchange Commission (SEC) requires all publicly listed companies to disclose information that may affect the share price of the company, such as the shareholding structure, or a change in the inside shareholding. This can give the intelligent millennial investor a chance to research the top leadership of the individual companies they may be considering.

In my case, I look at the qualifications of the top leadership and their past record of accomplishment of leadership. If any of them have a questionable record of accomplishment or past scandals, I tend to stay away from those companies. I prefer to invest in companies with leaders who have integrity and a solid reputation. The executive team provides a general insight into the organization's management as they are the ones who make the big decisions that affect the company internally.

The management can also be assessed on how well they are managing the financial affairs of the company. The intelligent millennial investor can research company financial statements including Income Statements, Balance Sheets, and Cash Flow Statements to assess the financial position. All this financial information is publicly available to the intelligent millennial investor.

As a rule of thumb, companies that have extraordinarily strong financial positions are more likely to withstand shocks like the one experienced starting in mid-2022 when central banks in Canada and the US started increasing interest rates. I define a company

---

[55] https://www.ruleoneinvesting.com/toolbox/

with solid fundamentals if they have increasing cash flows relative to their long-term debt. I like businesses that can hypothetically pay off their long-term debt in at most 3 years if they were to clear it off. In addition, I prefer companies with a return on equity (ROE) of at least 15% a year, because when I invest my money, I like a good return. So, using screeners (software that can search through many stocks), I put the parameter of ROE of at least 15% a year.

An intelligent millennial investor can investigate the financial performance of a company for the past 10 years and see how revenue variables such as revenue, net income, debt, and cash on hand have been performing over time. While nobody can predict the future with certainty, past performance can provide a starting point. A simple approach is to follow the checklist of the margin of safety (the difference between the intrinsic value and the current stock price of a security), moat, and predictability of a security based on past records of financial performance. Once a stock satisfies all the boxes noted above, an intelligent millennial investor can put it on a watch list and wait for the price to drop below the intrinsic value. In other words, if a stock is undervalued, and the business I want to invest in has values that align with my personal values, and they have competitive advantage, I can consider investing in it, only when it is valued at a discounted price.

4. Margin of safety

A margin of safety is the difference between the true value and the sticker price of a security, such as a stock. The bigger the margin of safety the better for the intelligent millennial investor. Investing in the stock market requires a lot of discipline and patience. Hence if one can get in at a good price with a good margin of safety, the short-term price fluctuations will have minimal impact on the value of the investment. A margin of safety can be obtained if the security is priced below the intrinsic value (undervalued). The stock can be underpriced for various reasons, including negative news about the business, or missing an earnings target. The drop in stock price is usually temporary and short term. Sometimes there may be negative investor sentiment after key events such as missing earnings targets or macroeconomic events such as increase in policy rates by the Federal Reserve Bank.

The stock market has been shown to be mostly driven by valuation, sentiment, and profits in the long term.[56] Also, in the long term, the stock market adjusts the price of securities to equilibrium. This means as soon as there is news about a certain stock, investors usually rush to buy or sell until there are no more players willing to transact the security as soon as possible to ensure efficiency of the market.

On the other hand, it is worth mentioning that the stock market contains a fraction of the companies that constitute the whole economy. For example, the SPX constitutes 80% of the US Gross Domestic Product (GDP). Most people tend to confuse the stock market and the entire economy.

When COVID-19 hit in 2020, it presented another huge opportunity for stocks to be undervalued as most investors panicked and sold off their shares. This is another great example where a huge margin of safety can be created for the intelligent millennial investor. The key is to do your homework and research ahead of time. By identifying exceptionally good businesses that satisfy the four checklists (Four M's) and keeping them on a watch list. In my case, I use different tools such as going to the company website, checking their filings with the SEC, and tool boxes like the Rule one that collates all the publicly available information about the company in real time. In addition, websites such as yahoo finance and google finance also provide key information for financial statement and business events such as earnings dates etc. That is when patience pays. Just wait and wait until a significant event happens and jump in when everyone in the crowd is rushing to sell good businesses.

In addition, to ensure a maximum return, the intelligent millennial investor should always ensure that they buy a security for a discount price; that is, below the intrinsic value.

---

[56]https://shorturl.at/jBT59.

Hence, for an intelligent millennial investor to receive a higher return, one must do some valuations and make sure that they pay for a value that is lower than the intrinsic value of a security, as it is believed that the stock will always revert to the intrinsic value over the long term. There are various ways to value securities, such as the Discounted Cash Flow Model I explained in the Meaning section. However, most of the information that is needed to value a stock is publicly available, and there are even calculators that are widely available online that can be used to calculate a stock's price. An example is the Fair Value Calculator[57] but one must subscribe and pay for the data.

The global economy is overly complicated as it is driven by many variables, some of which are beyond the control of individuals. In the short term, the stock market has been shown to be influenced by many factors that include investor sentiment, valuations of securities, interest rates, government policy and geopolitics.[58] As a result, it is hard for an intelligent millennial investor to accurately predict the direction of either the stock market in the short term or the global economy.

The intelligent millennial investor can take advantage of these huge market corrections and buy more to hold long term. The key is to have a long term strategy and stay with it even in times of uncertainty. Hence it is important not to be influenced by short-term market fluctuations. Perhaps the best idea is to buy low and simply refrain from looking at the brokerage account for a while, at least until the dust settles, to avoid panicking and selling.

In general, most mutual fund managers do a good job managing investors' funds. However, they charge high fees which end up failing to beat the passively managed ETFs

---

[57]https://valueinvesting.io/fair-value-calculator.
[58]https://www.theglobeandmail.com/investing/education/article-should-i-invest-now-or-wait-for-a-correction/.

such as SPY and many others with low fees such as VOO managed by Vanguard. One could just buy a few highly liquid and well diversified index funds, a few individual stocks that meet the investment criterion described above (the Four M's) and hold for the long term. That way one would at least be guaranteed a benchmark return over the long term, as we have seen over the past decades. One does not need to hold a lot of securities to make money. A well-diversified portfolio would perform the magic of building wealth over the long term.

Another interesting question is whether one should keep cash in the bank when the opportunity cost of doing so could be negative. The answer to the question is not straightforward. The intelligent millennial investor could benefit from having some part of their net worth in cash. The cash can be kept in a high-interest-yielding digital bank with low fees. In Canada, Tangerine and Equity Bank are quite popular.

In addition, banks provide a safe option for holding cash if the financial system is well regulated. In Canada for example, there is a very robust oversight by the Financial Consumer Agency of Canada and various provincial- and federal-level regulators. Most bank money managers have been shown to sell at the bottom of the bear market due to fear, especially if it persists for a long time, instead of taking advantage of the dips in the market. One possible explanation could be that these managers are trying to reduce short-term loss in returns that may affect their performance bonuses. Of course, there are some particularly good and ethical bank managers who have integrity.

As a rule of thumb, an intelligent millennial investor might wish to have about 20 percent of their portfolio in cash, usually kept in short-term money market accounts that are readily accessible should the need arise. This can be used to take advantage of potential market corrections. Note that the 20 percent should be over and above the emergency fund because an intelligent millennial investor should never put themselves in a situation where they would have to sell their securities in the stock market to cater to emergency needs. The emergency fund is for emergencies.

Holding cash in the bank may seem like a loss of the potential to make money in the market. However, in his classic book published in 2020, *The Psychology of Money*, Morgan Housel raises an exceptionally good point about the advantage of keeping part of one's net worth in cash. The corrections in the stock market are unknown, at least in the short term. I doubt anyone could have known when the global stock market would crash due to the COVID-19-induced lockdowns worldwide. However, over the years research has shown that on average, negative returns in the stock market happen once every four years.[59]

The intelligent millennial investor can focus on variables they can control and consider what they cannot control. The intelligent millennial investor can control the frequency of investing their money in the market and the multiple streams of income they can earn. Timing the market therefore is a situation where one waits for the market to bottom out, perhaps because of a market correction, and then starts to invest. The challenge with this approach is that nobody really knows when the next market correction will happen; further, most people find it psychologically challenging to invest when everyone is selling off, and so they will hold the cash position until the market is back to the peak.

Even so-called pundits agree that timing the corrections is difficult. As an example of timing the market corrections, consider what happened in 2009 when the stock market dropped by 37 percent. Purchasing at that low point would guarantee that when the stock market recovered—as it always has done in the long term—a better rate of return on investment could be realized.

While holding cash in a chequing account or short-term money account may seem like one is losing out, behavioral psychology has shown that the human brain can mislead us much of the time. In his 2011 book, *Thinking Fast and Slow,* author and Nobel Laureate Daniel Kahneman points out that the human mind has two thought processes, *System 1,*

---

[59]https://www.thebalance.com/stock-market-returns-by-year-2388543.

and *System 2*. System 1 is usually the one that gets activated when there is an emergency situation, and it is fast, instinctive, and emotional. For example, when the stock market drops and one has some money invested, instead of doing the rational thing—that is, to buy more for those who have long positions—most people sell at this point due to fear.

On the other hand, *System 2* is often characterized by slower reactions and a more thoughtful and rational thought process. The problem is that most of the time, people act on impulse and based on the general sentiment of the majority, as aptly pointed out by William Bernstein in his 2021 book *The Delusions of Crowds.* The book explains why people generally follow a herd mentality when making decisions, even to the detriment of their individual interests. And this may explain why some people speculate even though the odds of winning are low; it is also one reason the intelligent millennial investor should rethink when making investment decisions—because the human brain can trick us. In all these situations, the intelligent millennial investor should always ask *What if I am wrong?* This can help crystallize their thoughts. The intelligent millennial investor can consider having a rule-based investing strategy to help in certain situations, such as those described below. The rule-based investing strategy may be in the form of a *heuristic*.

A heuristic is a mental shortcut that allows people to make quick decisions based on predetermined premises. As an example, after thoroughly researching their investment strategy, the intelligent millennial investor may have a heuristic that is informed by empirically tested theory. The global economy usually moves in cycles; sometimes different regions may have different growth rates because of different geopolitical issues and various shocks. An example is the COVID-19 vaccination rollout: because most of the vaccine manufacturing factories are based in the Global North, the Global South may witness a slow recovery compared to the United States and Canada, whose economies are ahead in terms of vaccination rates.

The intelligent millennial investor may therefore choose an index fund that has a higher weighting in the developing countries like South Africa, Brazil, and India. The Emerging Shares MSCI Emerging Markets ETF (EEM) is an example of an index that has exposure to emerging markets. The intelligent millennial investor can then have a rule-based investing strategy such as this: for every drop of at least five percent in any of these index funds, add shares. Alternatively, one can have an automated investing strategy where with every paycheck deposited, the bank automatically deducts a preset amount into a predetermined security. I prefer to buy on a red day, that is, when the market is low, so I do not even log into my brokerage account every day. I only log in when I want to specifically invest or check something important. Most of my time I spend reading and working to increase multiple streams of earnings.

Key Issues to consider when designing a winning investment strategy

1. Create a financial plan

A financial plan, as indicated in Chapter 1, can take the form of a simple written budget to show you how you can control your spending and achieve other goals such as increasing savings and investing rates and paying off debts if one has any. This can help create a solid foundation for gaining full awareness of one's financial affairs.

2. Get an education

Education has been long touted as a pathway to success. It can advance the prospects of obtaining higher-paying jobs. An education opens possibilities and job markets—where you will be paid to think; employers are essentially 'renting' your knowledge. Also, having specific knowledge can enable one to charge a higher rate compared to the prevailing market rates.

To be rich, one must leverage their specific knowledge to create something that is needed by society and not yet available. Elon Musk was able to figure out that climate change would be a big issue before most people did and started Tesla, which presently has a market capitalization of over US$640 billion. Society has handsomely rewarded him as one of the richest people on earth with his network increasing by US$205.5 billion in 2024 alone.[60]

Fortunately, many millennials also started educating themselves about investing after the COVID-19 pandemic forced them to stay indoors. There are a lot of investing courses available, and personal finance education can include reading books extensively as well as taking online courses. I was lucky to have a strong background in economics, and I have also taken online courses including a valuable course on investing by Philip Town[61]. This three-day course cost US$500, but it opened a whole new world to me. There are also many valuable low-cost and no-cost investing courses available online.

3. Create multiple income streams

Having multiple income streams is a great starting point. Full-time jobs are a great thing to have and can also help provide steady income for those starting a part time business on the side. This was explained in greater detail in Chapter 2.

4. Choose an investing strategy and consider your risk tolerance

Investing and trading are two different things. One can decide to use a fund manager or take the DIY approach to money management. The intelligent millennial investor may consider a hybrid model, a mix of a few high-quality, low-fee and broadly diversified index funds and a few very fundamentally strong companies that can be bought at a discount.

The intelligent millennial investor may consider consistently buying index funds each time the market drops and when funds are available, and then have a portion of cash available in a liquid money market account, ready to deploy when the individual companies one monitors drop to a good margin of safety. A money market account is an interest-bearing deposit account that allows individuals to earn a higher interest rate compared to

---

[60]https://shorturl.at/kIL47.
[61]https://shorturl.at/ekCMZ.

traditional savings accounts. It typically offers check-writing privileges and may provide a debit card for easy access to funds.

Historically, company share prices fluctuate if there is news or some catalyst such as earnings miss reports. Patience is always essential if one wants to invest in individual stocks. A simple rule of thumb I use is to just rebalance my portfolio and take risk up to a point where I can sleep peacefully without worrying about losing the money.

One way to look at it is to consider this question: If there is a drop in the market, could I tolerate it? Investing is easy and exciting when the stock market is going up, but it is psychologically challenging to watch share values drop in a bear market. A bear market is generally defined as a decline of 20% or more in stock prices from recent highs as measured by the major index such and the SPX and DJI. This decline is often accompanied by negative investor sentiment and a pessimistic outlook for the economy. Bear markets can be triggered by various factors, including economic downturns, geopolitical events, financial crises, or changes in market sentiment. The specific cause of a bear market can vary, but it often involves a combination of factors that erode investor confidence and lead to selling pressure.

A bear market is the opposite of a bull market, which is characterized by rising stock prices and positive investor sentiment. Bull and bear markets are part of the natural market cycle and can alternate over time. Currently the SPX and DJI reached their all-time high meaning, there has been a bull run. I like to keep some cash over and above my emergency fund to take advantage of stock market drops.

5. Rebalance the portfolio as needed

Rebalancing is an important issue to consider on this wealth-building journey. While it is a good thing to consider diversifying asset allocation, for example into real estate, gold, stocks, and bonds, it is also important to consider buying more of the prices of securities that are dropping and in some cases even selling securities that have become overweighted in relation to the rest of your portfolio and moving the proceeds to positions that have become underweighted.

Traditionally, most experts recommend holding a 60/40 ratio of stocks to bonds depending on the stage of life of the investor. As people get older, they tend to need more income and as they mostly stop working, they will need more income to cater for their living expenses. Also, as people get older, they may not have as much time to wait for the stock market to recover without suffering a big dent on their income streams. So, a portfolio with a mix of both equities and bonds tends to offer better stability of returns.

So, a 60/40 portfolio refers to an investment strategy that allocates 60% of the portfolio to stocks and 40% to bonds. This allocation is a common approach used by investors seeking a balance between growth potential and stability.

Here are some key points about the 60/40 portfolio:

a) Allocation

A 60/40 portfolio typically consists of 60% stocks and 40% bonds. The stock allocation aims to provide growth potential and capital appreciation, while the bond allocation offers stability and income generation. I like to also hold ETFs that track the volatility index which normally cushions me when the market drops. At a given time, I like to have about 10% of my portfolio in the bonds and ETFs that track the VIX index. The VIX Index is the CBOE Volatility Index which popularly measures market volatility of the stock market.

Theoretically, bonds and stocks usually move in opposite directions. So, having a combination of bonds and stocks can help in managing the potential risk of losing everything in the stock market. I am relatively young, and I like to take more risk, so I hold more stocks than bonds, above the recommended ratio. The portfolio composition will change over time as I grow older.

6.   Consider your stage of life

As I stated in previous paragraphs, a portfolio for a millennial and a near retiree may be quite different as they are at different points in life. For a near retiree, a conservative portfolio would be ideal, while an intelligent millennial investor is able to consider more risk and will likely have time to recover from a market drop.

7.   Understand the tax code in your country of residence and optimize taxes!

It seems many people become angry when they read articles discussing how the rich pay little or no tax by taking advantage of tax loopholes. Tax is an instrument that governments all over the world employ to transfer wealth across the economy and pay for public goods such as defense and healthcare. Tax can take many different forms, such as income tax, property tax and the silent one, inflation tax. Income tax is that portion the government deducts from one's income while property tax is a levy on the value of a property. Inflation tax accounts for the loss in real value of money due to factors such as government printing money or other reasons. That means keeping money as cash in the bank can result in loss of value if the inflation rate is going up.

Rather than being angry at the rich who take advantage of their knowledge and tax loopholes, the intelligent millennial investor can consult a tax attorney or read about taxation. It is possible to save money by simply understanding how to legally avoid paying taxes. Please note the emphasis on *legally* avoiding tax. This means paying no more than is legally required. There are situations where people evade tax, and this is simply not worth the risk.

Sooner or later, the tax authorities will find out and there are heavy penalties for tax evaders. Also, it is morally wrong in my view to not pay one's fair share of taxes. For example, in Canada we have the Canada Revenue Agency (CRA) to monitor taxes. All banks and financial institutions report to CRA; hence they have access to all transactions that move through the financial system. It is a fool's errand to evade taxes; do not do it!

In Canada, there are vehicles that can be used to optimize taxes, including various registered accounts such as the registered accounts as I have explained in the first chapter.

Chapter 7: Portfolio diversification

One of the key lessons I have learnt as a retail investor over the past four years investing in the US and Canadian stock exchanges, is that diversification and meaning risk are important to succeed in investing. Hence diversification and managing risk and it can be the difference between success or failure as an investor. As investing comes with inherent risk that I have described in chapter 7, when an investor diversifies on the securities they own, it can potentially spread the risk.

Portfolio diversification is when an investor spreads their investments across different asset classes, sectors, regions, or types of securities to reduce risk and potentially enhance returns. The goal of diversification is to build a portfolio of asset classes that are not overly reliant on the performance of a single investment or asset. In other words, I invest in equities, bonds, and hold some cash over and above the emergency fund. To provide more connection to diversification, I explain the main principles that come with good diversification of investment portfolio.

a) Risk management

 Diversification in itself is a risk management strategy that aims to reduce the impact of any individual investment's poor performance on the overall portfolio. By diversifying my portfolio, I can potentially reduce the risk associated with a specific company, industry, or market segment underperforming or in an extreme case by way of bankruptcy.

b) Asset allocation

Diversification can be achieved through asset allocation, which involves dividing investments among different asset classes such as stocks, bonds, cash, real estate, or commodities. Each asset class has its own risk and return characteristics, and their performance may vary under different market conditions. In building my portfolio, I invest in a few individual stocks that pass on the checklists of my investment criterion I explain in the previous chapter, and then buy a few ETFs that track the major Indexes such as SPX in the US. As my own rule, I do not like to invest more than 10% of my overall portfolio in one individual stock, regardless of how confident I am because there is a possibility that any business can fail. So, I limit my risk that way too. I also invest in bonds through ETFs, and I like to also buy a few ETFs that track the volatility Index. When the market is volatile, such as the VIX Index, it shows that the market is very volatile and hence, that way, it can potentially cushion me in such a scenario. Unlike being all in equities, diversification can protect my portfolio from extreme fluctuations.

In terms of allocating some money in bonds, I prefer to put a small fraction of my portfolio in bonds. Bond yields generally move in opposite directions to those of equities, especially in a period of a recession. A recession is often a situation when the economy's major sectors register a marked decline in output for at least three consecutive months. In addition, even when the stock prices move in the same directions, bonds are less volatile to equities such as stocks. This is particularly important because if one is in retirement, selling shares in their portfolio might hit their portfolio hard. So, bonds can come in handy.

I also like to own some fixed income securities such as treasury bills and Guaranteed Investment Certificates (GICs). Fixed income securities are debt instruments issued by governments, corporations, or other entities to finance their operations. For example, the government of Canada through the Bank of Canada can issue treasury bills for a yield and sell to the public. These securities provide investors with a fixed periodic payment, typically in the form of interest, and the return of the principal amount at maturity. They are considered a way to achieve a diversified portfolio while offering a secure, low-risk way to generate a steady flow of income. Generally, banks often have Treasury bills as a part of their assets because they are guaranteed if held to maturity. Unlike stock which may fluctuate in price over time.

Examples of fixed income securities include bonds, treasury bills, GICs, mortgages, or preferred shares. These securities represent a loan by the investor to the issuer. The payments of fixed income securities are known in advance, providing a guaranteed return on investment if held to maturity. Fixed income securities are often favored by investors, particularly retirees, who seek a predictable cash flow and a lower level of risk compared to other investments. They are considered to be relatively safe investments, as they offer capital preservation and a steady source of income. However, it is important to note that fixed income securities are not without risks, such as inflation risk, interest rate risk, and credit risk. I explained these risks in the preceding chapter.

Investors can diversify their portfolios by including fixed income securities alongside other asset classes, such as stocks or real estate. This diversification helps reduce the overall risk of the portfolio and provides stability during market fluctuations.

It is worth noting that fixed income securities can be purchased directly or through various investment vehicles such as exchange-traded funds (ETFs) or mutual funds. These investment options provide investors with access to a diversified portfolio of fixed income securities.

Hence, depending on my financial goals at that time, GICs offer some stability in that I would at least get my principal invested plus some interest to cushion from inflation. GICs can range from short to long term maturity and as short as a month and years. As an example, banks in Canada often offer GICs. Equity Bank has a wide range of GICs ranging up to 5 years for 4.35% interest on February 13, 2024[62].

In Canada, there are quite a few bonds also that are issued by municipal, provincial, and federal governments, and they offer some yield. The good thing is that, If I buy a bond from the federal government of Canada, I would be lending my money to the government and will get some interest on maturity. The downside is that most of the bonds require a minimum of $5,000 Canadian to open a position. The federal bonds when I called my

---

[62] https://www.eqbank.ca/personal-banking/investments/gics. Accessed on February 13, 2024.

broker the other day informed me they accept a minimum of $50, 000 to open a position for Treasury bills in Canada. So, that could be a barrier to some retail investors.

In addition, I also like to keep at least 20% of my overall portfolio in cash saved up in high-yield savings accounts. Even though in periods of rapid inflation like 2022 and part of 2023, inflation was high in Canada and the US, closing the year at about 3.4%[63]. In Canada, it has some merits to have cash. Holding cash can offer massive opportunities if the stock market suddenly falls and if one knows the stocks they want to invest in, that could be a huge opportunity to buy. In some cases, if one is planning to buy a house in a year, it might make sense to keep the money in GICs or cash because investing the money in the stock market might be risky. The stock market can be volatile, and it can drop at any time. So, one will not have control over when it can go back up again.

c) Sector and industry diversification

Different sectors and industries perform differently. As an example, the year 2023, the technology sector started the year in bear territory and most fundamentally good businesses such as Amazon, Google and Microsoft dropped by about 30% in the first quarter. However, as the year progressed as the federal reserve toned down on the rate hikes, they recovered and closed the year on a high note. This upward movement has continued into the January 2024, and has seen these technology stocks driving the major indices such as the SPX and DJI up to record high levels.

Hence, within each asset class, diversification can be further achieved by investing in different sectors or industries. This helps reduce the risk associated with a particular sector's performance. For example, my portfolio that includes investments in technology, healthcare, and consumer goods sectors may be less susceptible to the performance of a single sector. I also achieve this diversification by investing in ETFs that mimic the SPX.

---

[63] https://wowa.ca/inflation-rate-canada-cpi.

This gives me exposure to all sectors contained in the ETF such as technology, healthcare, financials, retail etc.

d) Geographic diversification

Geographic diversification involves investing in different regions or countries. This strategy helps reduce the risk associated with a specific country's economic or political events. By spreading investments globally, investors can potentially benefit from the growth of different economies and reduce exposure to any single market. In some cases, big companies that are multinational corporations such as Apple and Microsoft operate in different geographic regions. Apple has factories in China, Europe, and most other parts of the world. Each time I look at their financial statements, I notice that some of the business revenues come from outside of the US. In some cases, it can cushion the overall business revenue base when the US economy is not doing very well. So, this is the advantage.

There are years when other countries around the world grow faster than others owing to different factors. This can be useful to the overall portfolio. Other geographic areas to potentially invest in may include other developed countries, emerging economies such as China and other developing countries. I tend to stick to Canada and the US because I am more familiar with how their public markets work. I also invest in corporations that I mentioned which may have exposure intentionally. Berkshire Hathaway has some international investments which gives me some exposure to those areas they invest in. Even the SPX will be geographically diversified even though its headquarters are in the US. Some companies in the S&P 500 have exposure to other countries.

e) Security selection

Diversification can also be achieved through security selection within each asset class. For example, in the stock market, investors can diversify by investing in a mix of large-cap, mid-cap, and small-cap stocks, as well as across different industries. The benefit of diversification aims to reduce the overall risk of a portfolio without sacrificing potential returns. It helps smooth out the volatility of investment returns and provides a more stable long-term investment strategy. Diversification can also help capture opportunities in different market conditions and reduce the impact of market downturns.

It is however important to note that diversification does not guarantee profits or protect against losses, and it cannot eliminate the risk of investment. However, it is considered a fundamental principle of prudent investing.

f) Diversification by growth or value

There are two common investment styles namely value and growth-oriented investing strategy.

(i) Value-oriented investment style

Value-oriented investment style is an approach to investing that focuses on identifying undervalued securities and holding them for the long term. This means, an investor should look for stocks or other securities that are trading at a price below their intrinsic value. Investors using this style believe that the market may have overlooked or undervalued these securities, presenting an opportunity for potential gains when the market price goes back to the true value of the security.

One key investment thesis value investor usually follows when applying this approach is to pick companies with strong fundamentals, such as low price-to-earnings (P/E) ratios, low price-to-book (P/B) ratios, or high dividend yields. They aim to buy these securities at a discount price and hold them until the market recognizes their true value.

In addition, value investors usually invest in securities with a long-term focus. That is, they usually buy the stocks at a discounted price and hold them for a long time until they go to their intrinsic value. Hence, value investors expect that over time, the market will recognize the value of the securities they hold, leading to price appreciation. A well-known value investor is Warren Buffet who manages Berkshire Hathaway Corporation. He claims he follows lessons he learned from the popular book by Benjamin Graham, entitled, "The intelligent investor." Value investors should have patience and a willingness to hold investments for an extended period as a key virtue.

In addition, value investors apply a contrarian approach to their investments. This means they usually take a view that is different to the majority of investors based on their understanding of the businesses they will be investing in and go against the prevailing market sentiment. In doing so, they often invest in companies or sectors that are out of favor or facing temporary challenges, with the belief that the market will eventually recognize their value.

An important principle for value investors is to invest when they have a margin of safety (MOS). This refers to the difference between the intrinsic value of a security and its market price. Value investors seek securities with a significant MOS, which helps protect against potential losses if their assessment of the security's value is incorrect. A conclusion remark on value investing is that it is key to invest in only those businesses one understands and do a thorough research to understand the business fundamentals and including how the management is managing the business.

(ii) Growth-oriented investment style

Growth-oriented investment style is an approach to investing that focuses on selecting and investing in companies or securities that have the potential for above-average growth in earnings or value. To do so, growth-oriented investors identify companies or securities that are expected to experience rapid earnings growth or appreciation in value. Investors using this style believe that these companies have the potential to deliver significant returns over time. This can include start-ups that may have been listed through the Initial Public Offering (IPOs). An Initial Public Offering (IPO) is a process through which a privately owned company offers its shares to the public for the first time, making them available for purchase on a stock exchange.

Growth-oriented investors usually look for companies with strong growth prospects, such as those in emerging industries or with innovative products or services. They focus on metrics like revenue growth, earnings growth, and future growth potential rather than current valuation metrics. In some cases, they may even invest in IPOs that may not yet make profits. This can be a risky move if the business does not grow and on the upside, it can pay off hugely if it then grows. The big businesses we see today around the world were once IPOs, but the challenge is to identify them at an early stage.

In addition, growth-oriented investors invest with a long-term focus in mind. Growth-oriented investing is often considered a long-term strategy. Investors expect that over time, the companies they invest in will continue to grow and generate higher earnings, leading to an increase in the value of their investments.

Risk and volatility are a key characteristic for growth-oriented investments investors. Companies with high growth potential may experience significant price fluctuations as market expectations change. It is important for investors to have a higher risk tolerance and a longer investment horizon when pursuing a growth-oriented strategy. In this case, it is important for millennial investors to build an optimal emergency fund to ride out the volatility before the investments make profit.

Growth-oriented investors usually select businesses with a competitive advantage, strong management teams, and a record of accomplishment of delivering consistent growth. They may also consider factors such as industry trends, market share, and technological advancements when selecting investments.

The other characteristic for growth-oriented investors is diversification. I have explained diversification is still important in a growth-oriented portfolio. While growth investors may focus on specific sectors or industries with high growth potential, it's important to spread investments across different companies to reduce risk.

It is worth noting that growth-oriented investing, like any investment strategy, carries risks. Not all growth stocks or companies will meet expectations, and there is always the possibility of losses. Conducting thorough research and analysis is crucial when selecting securities for a growth-oriented portfolio. The few stocks that then become profitable and go up can be hugely rewarding.

g) Diversification across sectors

A popular way to diversify for some investors has been buying Index or ETFs. The index may own stocks invested in the different sectors or geographic regions. These can then cushion the overall performance of the fund in periods when other sectors or geographic regions are not performing well in terms of returns. In Canada and the US, there are major sectors such as financials, energy, technology, communication services, industrial stocks, real estate, utilities, consumer staples, consumer discretionary and materials.

An investor can also own individual stocks in different sectors, and it helps when other sectors are not doing well, the sectors that are doing well can then provide a better return. Some investors can also buy mutual funds which own different stocks across different sectors. In 2023, those invested in the Information Technology sector earned the highest return of about 56%. There are some years when these sectors rotate so, on average, it helps to have a well-diversified portfolio to get a much higher return over the long term.

Table 7.0 Showing returns for 2023 across different sectors in the United States

Rank	S&P Sector	2023 Return (%)
1	Information technology	56.4
2	Communication services	54.4
3	Consumer discretionary	40.3
4	Industrials	16
5	Materials	10.2
6	Financials	9.9
7	Real estate	8.3
8	Health care	0.3
9	Consumer staples	-0.23
10	Energy	-4.8
11	Utilities	-10.4

Source: www.visualcapitalist.com

Chapter 8: Estate planning

When I was growing up in my native Zimbabwe, it was common to see families fighting after the breadwinner passed on. Unfortunately, if the breadwinner left a family and kids behind, they would often face an uncertain future. As simple as it may seem to most people, few are comfortable discussing and planning for their deaths.

About six years ago, I had dinner with some close family friends in Canada. I was surprised to learn that they had already built a trust fund for their grandkids; children who were not yet born. After dinner, I had time to self-introspect. Of course, at some point we all shall die. However, the thought of planning for the allocation of wealth to the survivors has always intrigued me. It is important for an individual to have a mechanism and means of distributing wealth when one eventually leaves this earth.

For two years, I happened to be on the board of advisors for a non-profit organization representing the Zimbabwean community in British Columbia. Throughout the duration of my term as a director, I noticed that on a few occasions when a member of the community passed, there were financial challenges around how to repatriate the body of the deceased. I noticed that in those cases, the deceased did not have life insurance or the financial resources to cover the funeral costs which can be quite high in Canada, particularly if the deceased will have to be flown back to Zimbabwe. Fortunately, with the guidance of the leadership of the non-profit, there have been greater discussions and encouragement for the Zimbabwean community members to ensure they buy insurance policies.

On the other hand, having a will is important. A will, which is also known as a last will and testament, is a legal document that outlines how an individual would like their property and other assets to be distributed after their death. It allows a person to specify who will inherit your belongings and can also be used to nominate guardians for your children, dependents, or pets.

When creating a will, there are a few important terms to be aware of:

    a) Testator: The person who creates the will.

    b) Executor: The person appointed by the testator to carry out the instructions in the will.

    c) Beneficiaries: The individuals or organizations named in the will to receive specific assets or bequests.

    d) Probate: The legal process by which a will is proven in court and accepted as a valid public document, or the process by which an estate is settled according to the laws of intestacy in the absence of a legal will.

In my upbringing, I noticed that there has been a common misconception that one needs to be rich to have a will. Certainly, as one starts to build wealth, it is important to have a will. A good starting point is to look for templates online or consult a lawyer to get help drafting a will.

There are different types: The will can be a formal will, which is one that can just be drawn up by a notary public rather than a lawyer. There is also the holographic will, which is a handwritten version that is dated, signed by the beholder. In this case, there is no witness to countersign for the holographic will[64]. The Law Depot website provides templates one can customize as they wish.

Then, some people create trusts which formalize the assets and liabilities for people or businesses in question. So, a trust is a legal arrangement that allows a third party, known as a trustee, to hold assets on behalf of one or more beneficiaries. Trusts can be structured in various ways and can specify how and when the assets will be distributed to the beneficiaries. They are commonly used in estate planning to manage and protect assets, provide for loved ones, and minimize taxes.

---

[64]https://shorturl.at/CFJP5.

Types of trusts

There are different types of trusts that serve various purposes. Some common types include:

a) Revocable Living Trust: This type of trust can be changed or revoked by the grantor during their lifetime. It allows assets to be transferred outside of probate, potentially providing privacy, and avoiding the need for court involvement.

b) Irrevocable Trust: Once established, an irrevocable trust generally cannot be modified or revoked without the consent of the beneficiaries. It can offer potential tax benefits and asset protection, as the assets are no longer considered part of the grantor's estate.

c) Testamentary Trust: Created through a will, a testamentary trust goes into effect after the grantor's death. It allows for the distribution of assets to beneficiaries according to the terms specified in the will.

d) Charitable Trust: This type of trust is established to benefit charitable organizations or causes. It can provide tax advantages for the grantor while supporting philanthropic endeavors. Wealthy families often create these kinds of trusts. Examples can be the Bill and Melinda Foundation.

So, as a millennial investor, it may be worthwhile to consider having a trust as your wealth grows. As I have noted earlier on, failure to create a will can cause problems for those who are left behind. All too often I have seen people, particularly in the African communities among my connections, using GoFundMe platforms to raise money to cover funeral costs.

Let me be clear: There is nothing wrong with this, but the stress associated with fundraising during a time of mourning can be avoided by purchasing an insurance policy that is activated upon the death of the policy holder. Sometimes this is available as an employee benefit through work, which helps.

In addition, for those based in Canada, the CPP does provide a death benefit. The CPP death benefit is a one-time, lump-sum payment made to the estate or other eligible individuals on behalf of a deceased CPP contributor. The amount of the death benefit is up to a maximum of $2,500. To qualify for the death benefit, the deceased must have made contributions to the CPP for at least one-third of the calendar years in their contributory period, with a minimum of three calendar years, or a total of 10 calendar years.

If the CPP death benefit is approved, it would be typically paid to the estate, but if there is no estate or the executor has not applied for the benefit, it may be paid to other eligible individuals, such as the person responsible for paying funeral expenses or the surviving spouse or common-law partner. The application for the CPP death benefit can be made by completing the application for a Canada Pension Plan death benefit form and submitting it to Service Canada. The processing time for the death benefit payment is usually between 6 to 12 weeks. And a reminder, for government of Canada services and benefits, it is a good idea to apply for them through the official government website or in-person by visiting the respective government offices.

One family shared with me the story of what they went through when they lost their in-laws, and it was particularly challenging as an immigrant family in Canada. The family ended up having to borrow from the bank to cover the funeral costs—a stressful experience to go through. So, I urge the intelligent millennial investor to explore these options of creating a will and a trust to put their estate affairs in order. Death is an unavoidable fact of life for everyone.

In this book, I outline a strategy one can adopt to build wealth. This strategy involves first and foremost defining how much one will need for retirement. Then, assess what strategies can be taken to achieve this financial freedom number. The intelligent millennial investor may also optimize savings, after building a 6-12 months' worth of living expenses as an emergency fund. Do away with bad debt. Debt can drag you backwards. The bible says the borrower will always be the slave to the lender. Having a lot of debt also can be psychologically depressing.

Then, increase multiple streams of income by working full time or earn a high skill that can pay a good income, starting a business, or perhaps starting a side hustle for a few hours to increase the streams of income. On average wealthy people have multiple streams of income that may include royalties, dividends from investments, income streams from real estate properties and other investments. The bottom line is, they make their money from investments and not by trading their time for money.

Wealthy people also invest steadily over time, starting as early as possible to take advantage of the impact of compound interest. Most research on financial markets has shown that it is much harder than it seems to beat the benchmark index, the S&P index. So, does not it then make sense to just invest most of your income in index funds? Perhaps with a mixture of a few particularly good individual companies.

The reader may also choose to follow a simple hybrid investing strategy. That is, having most of their income invested in a few high-quality index funds, a smaller percentage invested in high-quality individual companies that meet the 4 M's outlined in this book, a small percentage invested in real estate, and the remaining 20 percent saved up as cash to take advantage of immediate cash needs and unexpected drops in the markets. The percentage of money invested in each part of the portfolio would depend on one's age and risk tolerance.

This portfolio composition can be adjusted as one grows older to increase the holding of index funds which have some level of diversification compared to investing in one individual business. Also, as one retires, cash needs and risk tolerance may change. The advantage of this hybrid strategy is that index funds are diversified, have low fees, and can provide a cushion while providing a decent return over the long term. The individual stocks may provide an option for a higher return that can be balanced out by the return from index funds. Some people automate their investments, that is, a portion of every paycheck is automatically deposited into their respective investments.

As Morgan Housel noted in his book, *The Psychology of Money*, if you want to be successful as an investor, the single most powerful thing you can do is to increase your time horizon. Then focus on what you can control. Investment variables you can control may include frequency of investment in securities of your choice and how much you invest. I know of a few friends who save up throughout the year, and then buy low when fund managers sell off most of their losing securities for tax harvesting in the tax seasons. Some may elect a dollar cost average.

Basically, automating to buy predetermined securities and regular intervals, regardless of the price changes. I normally like to buy consistently when stocks or indexes fall by a certain percentage (heuristics). For example, I buy index funds whenever the market drops by at least five percent. I do not try to time the market because nobody can do that with certainty. Even the so-called experts cannot predict the direction of the market with certainty. So, why waste your time on something that you do not have control over?

Learn to wait and be patient and invest in the right securities and commodities that one is comfortable with or at least knowledgeable about. To paraphrase a well-known adage, the problem with most poor people is that they want to live like the rich, when in fact, the rich live just like the poor. A case in point: many rich people buy good second-hand cars as opposed to brand new vehicles.

If you choose to marry, choose someone with whom your financial values align. And keep in mind that there are a lot of things that can provide joy and yet are free. Outside of my work-related activities, I love taking walks, watching educational material on YouTube, and reading good books. I like to read books that challenge conventional thinking, and I like to read about the experiences of others who have succeeded in their financial journeys.

The COVID-19 pandemic has also forced people worldwide to adopt virtual learning and meet-ups. This is cheaper than traveling for conferences. Being wealthy will enable you to gain back *control* over your time and pursue all the things that you want to, without the worry of working for money. In other words, you will have created a system that works for you and hence, your money will work for you, and not the other way around.

In conclusion, I am also aware that my worldview is not universal, so it is important to be you and choose to follow what makes you happy. I respect that people have choices. I do what works for me. Above everything else, I do my best to just live my life to the fullest and *always* take care of my mental wellbeing. There is no reason to keep postponing my happiness into the unforeseeable future. So, dear reader, consider spending some time figuring out what you love the most and do it whilst alive. Avoid ruinous risk and remember to pay taxes. Always.

Appreciation

In this life, there is so much for me to be grateful for. I have a wonderful wife, a lovely son and loving parents who have supported me through all the writing process. Some days were long, and my family tolerated me chasing my passion.

I am extremely grateful to Dr. Thomas W. Ross, someone who has become much more than my friend. Dr. Ross has provided extensive comments to my book despite his busy schedule.

I am grateful to Ruth-Anne, my editor whom I met at a park in Langley. Little did I know that she would provide me with extensive edits for this book. I really appreciate it.

I have also greatly benefited from discussions with friends and my family regarding financial experiences. The discussions we have had informed me about the general financial habits we all face as human beings when it comes to money. Foremost, my wife Isabel, Kuzi Mutonga, Blooming Umoren, Eddie Armaitum, Ally Sekora, Gladys Matava, Brian Mukweswe and Mercy Wanalo, thank you for being willing to share your insights on investing.

About the author

Isaac Jonas completed his undergraduate degree in economics at the University of Zimbabwe in 2010 before embarking on a journey to further his studies at the University of British Columbia (UBC), Canada. Academically equipped with a Master of Food and Resources Economics which he earned as a Mastercard Foundation Scholar before he also read for an M.A. in Resources, Environment and Sustainability, which he completed in May 2021.

Over the past several years, Isaac has worked as a manager, research and policy analyst, research assistant and a board member for several non-profits in Canada and Zimbabwe.

Most recently, Isaac joined the content creator economy where he has been regularly creating videos for publishing on YouTube on the topics around personal finance, investing and productivity. He consistently posts his content on YouTube platforms via the Streetwise Economics handle and on his social media platforms including LinkedIn, Meta Platforms (formerly Facebook) and X (formerly Twitter).

His mission is to share educational content on personal finance, investing and productivity with a wider audience. During his free time, he enjoys reading books and journals on finance, investment and productivity and traveling around the world, learning new cultures, and seeing new places. He is also currently working on his next book manuscript, Previously, he has authored a flagship book, *The Serendipity of a Great Network*, which narrates his journey from a small village in rural Zimbabwe to starting his academic journey in Canada in 2014. He has also created online educational materials which are available online. Isaac's educational content is available online via his website: www.streetwiseeconomics.com.

APPENDIX A

(CHAPTER 1)

A recap of the mathematics behind the four percent rule discussed in chapter 1 which is used to estimate the amount of money I would require to retire financially for a thirty-year period. The mathematical model is extracted from Kristy Shen and Bryce Leung's book, *Quit Like a Millionaire*. The four per cent rule they use as a maximum yearly withdrawal state that one can safely retire for thirty years with a balanced portfolio of stocks and bonds once their expenses equal four per cent of their portfolio.

$$0.04 \ X \ P = E$$

Where P is the portfolio size and E is the annual expenses. Expressing E in terms of one\s savings rate (S) and Income (I).

$$0.04 \ X \ P = I \ X \ (1 - S)$$

Expressing the portfolio in terms of Income and N years, assuming a return to the portfolio of r. r in this case is often referred to as the future value in economics and finance.

$$0.04 \ X \ I \ X \ S \left[\frac{(1 + r)^N - 1}{r} \right] = IX(\,1 - S)$$

Which simplifies to:

$$\left[\frac{(1+r)^N - 1}{r} \right] = 25 \ X \ \frac{(1-S)}{S}$$

Solving the equation further, we get:

$$N \ X \ Log \ (1 + r) = X \ r + 1$$

In the end, we get the following expression:

$$N \ = \ \frac{Log \, 25x \, [\dfrac{(1 - S)}{S} \ X \, r + 1]}{Log(1 + r)}$$

Thus, in the end, we can express that N becomes a function of two variables, the savings rate, and the annual rate of return of the portfolio, r. By plugging this formula into an excel spreadsheet, we can find the range for the variable S between 5% and 100%, as well as the variable r between 1% and 10%. This can be simplified into an excel spreadsheet and calculate the income level to be able to live off the proceeds of the investments.

Glossary

Bear market: a situation of the financial markets where prices are falling or are expected to fall for a sustained period.

Bull market: a situation of the financial markets where prices are rising or are expected to rise for a sustained period.

Dollar cost averaging: an investment strategy that involves buying investment securities such as stocks on a regular schedule and spending the same amount each time so that when prices fall you are buying more units and when prices rise you are buying fewer units.

Gross Domestic Product: total value added to the economy through the production and sale of goods and services within an economy over a fixed time, usually a year.

Heuristic: it is a simplified decision process (a short cut) that uses things like rules of thumb to get "good enough" answers.

Index Fund: a portfolio made up to match and track the components of the financial markets.

Intrinsic value: the true value of a security such as a stock after incorporating all fundamentals.

Investing: involves buying securities with the intention to hold for more than a year with the expectation of making a profit.

Margin call: happens when a margin account runs low on funds, generally because of a losing trade.

Margin of safety: the difference between the true value of a security and the sticker price.

Mutual fund: an investment program funded by shareholders that trades in diversified holdings and is professionally managed by a fund manager.

Option: a stock option that gives an investor a right, but not an obligation, to buy or sell stock at an agreed-upon time and date for a specified price. One option contract has one hundred underlying shares.

Security: a financial instrument that holds value and can be bought and sold between parties.

Specific education: a soft skill that enables one to develop a unique type of expertise in a certain field.

Swing trading: a type of trading that tries to capture the short- to medium-term gains of a security over a period of few days to several weeks.

Ticker name: a unique series of letters assigned to a security for trading purposes.

Trading: an economic concept which involves buying and selling of commodities and services, along with a compensation paid by a buyer to a seller.

List of Abbreviations

BC - British Columbia

CME – Chicago Mercantile Exchange

GDP – Gross Domestic Product

FOMO – Fear of Missing Out

MFRE – Master of Food and Resources Economics

SADC – Southern African Development Community

SEC – Securities and Exchange Commission

UBC – University of British Columbia

UZ – University of Zimbabwe

Cited Sources

1. A Jorgenson, E. (2021). *The Almanack of Naval Ravikant: A Guide to Wealth and Happiness.* Magrathea Publishing.

2. Bernstein, W. J. (2021). *The Delusions of Crowds: Why People Go Mad in Groups*. Grove Press.

3. Blanchett, D. (2023). Redefining the Optimal Retirement Income Strategy. *Financial Analysts Journal*, *79*(1), 5-16.

4. Kahneman, D, K. (2017). *Thinking, fast and slow*. Anchor Canada.

5. Mboweni, D (2020). A Dusty Road to Success: Principles of An Extraordinary Life.

6. Dimmock, S. G., Wang, N., & Yang, J. (2023). The endowment model and modern portfolio theory. *Management Science*.

7. Galloway, S. (2019). *The Algebra of Happiness: Notes on the Pursuit of Success, Love, and Meaning*. Penguin.

8. Galloway, S. (2021). *Post Corona*. Plataforma.

9. Graham, B. (1965). *The intelligent investor*. Prabhat Prakashan.

10. Grant, A. (2021). *Think Again: The Power of Knowing what You Don't Know*. Viking.

11. Housel, M. (2020). *The Psychology of Money: Timeless lessons on wealth, greed, and happiness*. Harriman House Limited.

12. Leung, B., & Shen, K. (2019). *Quit Like a Millionaire: No Gimmicks, Luck, or Trust Fund Required*. Hachette UK.

13. Malkiel, B. G. (2019). *A random walk down Wall Street: the time-tested strategy for successful investing*. WW Norton & Company.

14. Markowitz, H. M. (1991). Foundations of portfolio theory. *The journal of finance*, *46*(2), 469-477.

15. Mazur, M., Dang, M., & Vega, M. (2021). COVID-19 and the march 2020 stock market crash. Evidence from S&P1500. *Finance Research Letters*, *38*, 101690.

16. Ramsey, D. (2013). *The Total Money Makeover: Classic Edition: A Proven Plan for Financial Fitness*. Thomas Nelson.

17. Rieckens, S. (2019). *Playing with FIRE (Financial Independence Retire Early): How Far Would You Go for Financial Freedom?*. New World Library.

18. Robbins, T., & Mallouk, P. (2017). *Unshakeable: Your Financial Freedom Playbook*. Simon and Schuster.

19. Rob, B. (2023). Time to Retire: The 4% Withdrawal Rule. *The Journal of Investing*.

20. Sandberg, S., & Grant, A. (2017). *Option B*. Michel Lafon.

21. Thaler, R. H. (2015). *Misbehaving: The making of behavioral economics*. WW Norton & Company.